HMH

# JOURNEYS

# Write-In Reader

## Grade 5

Copyright © by Houghton Mifflin Harcourt Publishing Company

Printed in the U.S.A.

ISBN 978-0-547-87423-4

29 30 31   1468   21 20 19 18

4500703148     A B C D E F G

# Be a Reading Detective!

Welcome to your *Write-In Reader*! With this book, you will be a **Reading Detective**. You will look for clues in stories and in nonfiction selections. The clues will help you

▶ **enjoy stories,**

▶ **understand nonfiction,**

▶ **answer questions, and**

▶ **be a great reader!**

A Reading Detective can solve the mystery of any reading selection. No selection is too hard! A Reading Detective **asks questions**. A Reading Detective **reads carefully**.

Asking questions and reading carefully will help you **find clues**. Then, you will

▶ **stop,**

▶ **think, and**

▶ **write!**

## Let's try it! Follow the trail...

## Try It !

In the box is the beginning of a story. Read carefully. Ask yourself questions:

▶ **Who is the story about?**

▶ **Where and when does the story take place?**

▶ **What is happening?**

Look for clues to answer your questions.

> Logan was enjoying his bike ride. He felt the warm sun on his face. He smelled the beach nearby. He heard his dad humming on the bike in front of him. So far, Logan was having a great birthday.
>
> Suddenly, Logan screeched to a stop.
>
> "Dad!" he called out. "Look at that!"

**Stop** **Think** **Write**

Where and when does the story take place? How do you know?

_____

_____

Did you read carefully? Did you look for clues? Did the clues help you answer the questions? If they did, you are already a **Reading Detective**!

# Contents

interrupted
numb
specialty
staggered
struggled

# Different Kinds of Schools

**1** Throughout time, many families have **struggled** to pay for an education for their children. Families have an easier time in countries that have a system of free public schools.

**Write a word or words with the same meaning as struggled.**

_____

**2** One-room schoolhouses were common long ago. The room might have been heated by only a wood stove. Students' toes grew **numb** with cold. They would stamp their feet to get the feeling back in their toes.

**What might be a way to prevent numb feet?**

_____

_____

_____

**3** In parts of Australia, children live far from school. They learn by computer from home. Their education is never **interrupted** by bad weather. It only stops if a computer breaks down!

Tell about a time when your class was interrupted.

_____

_____

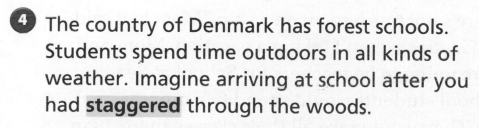

**4** The country of Denmark has forest schools. Students spend time outdoors in all kinds of weather. Imagine arriving at school after you had **staggered** through the woods.

Write a synonym for staggered.

_____

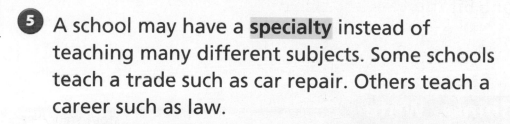

**5** A school may have a **specialty** instead of teaching many different subjects. Some schools teach a trade such as car repair. Others teach a career such as law.

What specialty would you like to learn?

_____

_____

_____

# An Ocean Learner

**by Laurie Rozakis**

Juan stared at the open cartons. How could he fit four months of his life into them? He had to, though. That was all Mom and Dad would let him take along.

"There's not much room on a ship," Mom had said.

The Garcias weren't taking a vacation. Mom and Dad were going to be teachers for School at Sea. High school students would spend two months on the ship. They would take all their classes there. Juan was going with his parents.

Mom and Dad were thrilled. Juan did not like the idea one bit.

| Stop | Think | Write |
| --- | --- | --- |

STORY STRUCTURE

**What problem does Juan have?**

_____

_____

_____

4

For weeks, the family prepared. They packed clothing, cameras, and books.

Mom and Dad spent hours writing lesson plans. Dad was a math teacher. Mom's **specialty** was science.

Juan spent the time complaining. "I am not a fish," he said. "I live on land. Why are you wrecking my life?"

"You'll love going to school at sea," said Mom. "You'll see how much you'll enjoy—"

Juan **interrupted** Mom before she could go on. "I want to go to *my* school. I don't want to be trapped on some boat."

## Stop Think Write

VOCABULARY

If you became a teacher, what <u>specialty</u> would you choose?

_____

_____

_____

5

Finally, the big day came. The Garcias arrived at the dock. Juan **staggered** unsteadily as he lugged a suitcase. Gripping the handle was making his fingers feel **numb**.

The ship was larger than Juan had expected. Maybe it wouldn't tip over and sink in a storm after all.

He wasn't going to be the only young kid on board. Another boy stood nearby. The other boy looked excited.

"That must be Ted Blake and his parents," said Dad.

"See?" said Mom. "You'll have friends. You're sharing a cabin with Ted."

Juan just grunted. He wanted his *land* friends.

**Stop** | **Think** | **Write**

**What is something else that can make someone's fingers feel <u>numb</u>?**

_____

_____

_____

Juan and Ted found their cabin. It was so tiny! The furniture was odd, too. The beds were built into the walls. Chairs were bolted to the floor. "Does this mean the boat could turn over on its side?" Juan asked.

"Not a chance," said Ted. "Big ships are pretty steady."

School began the next day. The teachers' kids had their own classes. There, Juan and Ted met Kim.

"What a great way to go to school," said Kim. "Here, when we study dolphins, we get to see them."

Dolphins? Juan loved dolphins. Maybe this ocean school would be okay.

**Stop | Think | Write**

STORY STRUCTURE

**How do Juan's feelings begin to change in this part of the story?**

_____

_____

_____

On the fourth day at sea, the three friends sat on the deck. They were doing homework. Suddenly, thunder boomed. Rain pounded onto the deck. High waves began to rock the ship. The friends hurried indoors. They **struggled** to walk steadily.

At last the three reached Juan and Ted's cabin. "Whew!" said Ted. "How could a storm come up that fast?"

Juan smiled. He knew the answer! "A warm front and a cold front came together," he said. "It was on the weather map we studied earlier."

"Cool!" said Kim. "We get to live what we're learning."

## Stop | Think | Write

**Why is the storm an important event in the story?**

_____

_____

_____

In a few hours, the sun had dried everything out. The three friends went back outside.

Mom came over. "Are you ready for science class?" she asked.

"We're way ahead of you," said Ted. "Our science class started hours ago."

For the first time in weeks, Juan felt like laughing, and he did. "Yes, Mom," he said. "We learned a thing or two about weather maps today."

Mom did not say "I told you so." She didn't have to. Juan had already figured out that he was going to a pretty good school.

## Stop   Think   Write

STORY STRUCTURE

Do you think Juan still has the same problem as before? Explain.

_____

_____

_____

## The World's Biggest Store: The Ocean!

We get more than just fish from the ocean. Sea plants and animals are used in medicine, toothpaste, shampoo, fertilizer, and ice cream.

## The Place to Live

More than half the people in the world live within sixty miles of an ocean. That is more than than 3.4 billion people! Close to half of all Americans live near the coast.

### Ocean Facts

| | |
|---|---|
| Area | The area of our oceans is 140 million square miles. That's more than two-thirds of Earth's surface. |
| Deepest point | The Mariana Trench in the western Pacific is more than five miles deep. |
| Biggest animal | The blue whale is the largest animal on Earth. It is bigger than the biggest dinosaur ever was. |

## Stop | Think | Write

MAIN IDEAS AND DETAILS

How do these facts help you understand more about what you can learn from going to school on a ship?

_____

_____

_____

# Look Back and Respond

**1** Which of the two settings is more important in this story? Why?

**Hint**

For clues, look at pages 4, 7, 8, and 9.

_____

_____

_____

**2** At first, how are Juan's feelings about School at Sea different from Ted's?

**Hint**

For clues, look at pages 4, 6, and 7.

_____

_____

_____

**3** How does Juan's attitude change during the story?

**Hint**

For clues, look at pages 5, 7, and 9.

_____

_____

_____

**4** What is the most important thing that Juan learns in the story?

**Hint**

For clues, look at pages 7, 8, and 9.

_____

_____

_____

# Be a Reading Detective!

**Return to**

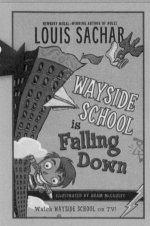

**1** Louis must deliver a package to Mrs. Jewls. What makes this problem even harder?

☐ The schoolyard is messy.

☐ Mrs. Jewls's room is on the thirtieth floor.

☐ There is no Mrs. Jewls.

"A Package for Mrs. Jewls" Student Book pp. 21–31

**Prove It!** What evidence in the story supports your answer? Check the boxes. ☑ Make notes.

| Evidence | Notes |
|---|---|
| ☐ what the narrator says | |
| ☐ Louis's words and feelings | |
| ☐ the illustrations | |

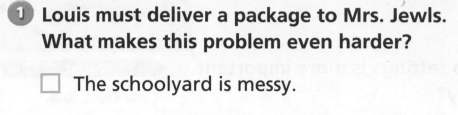

**Write About It!**

STORY STRUCTURE

Answer question **1** using evidence from the text.

_____

_____

_____

_____

_____

_____

_____

**2** **Louis thinks that the children love to work hard in school. Is he right?**

☐ yes ☐ no

☐ no way to know

**Prove It!** What evidence in the story supports your answer? Check the boxes. ☑ Make notes.

| Evidence | Notes |
|---|---|
| ☐ what happens on the playground | |
| ☐ what happens when Louis knocks | |
| ☐ what happens when the children see the computer | |
| ☐ | |

**Write About It!**

UNDERSTANDING CHARACTERS

**Answer question** **2** **using evidence from the text.**

_____

_____

_____

_____

_____

_____

**brandishing**
**bungled**
**discomfort**
**honored**
**interior**

# ON STAGE

**Check the answer.**

**1** If a play is set inside a house, then the play will take place in the _____ of the house.

☐ **exterior**      ☐ **attic**          ☐ **interior**

**2** In some of their plays, the actors of Shakespeare's company pretended to fight each other on stage, sometimes _____ fake swords.

☐ **bungling**    ☐ **brandishing**    ☐ **removing**

**3** The drama committee _____ the actress with a Best Supporting Actress award.

☐ **honored**    ☐ **brandished**    ☐ **disciplined**

**4** The actor pretended to yell in pain in order to show his character's _____.

☐ **interior**      ☐ **discomfort**      ☐ **joy**

**5** Describe a time when you were <u>honored</u> for an achievement.

_____

_____

_____

**6** How would you help a friend who felt <u>discomfort</u> in his or her stomach?

_____

_____

_____

**7** A friend feels that he or she <u>bungled</u> a school assignment. What would you say to make that friend feel better?

_____

_____

_____

# TWIN TWINS

## — BY JUSTIN SHIPLEY —

*Two best friends, Jamie and Kyle, head to the Little League World Series to see their favorite team, the Topeka Twins, play in the championship game.*

**Characters:** Jamie, Ms. Thompson, Kyle, Ticket Taker, Manager, Chase Conway

### SCENE I

*Setting: The interior of Ms. Thompson's car.*

**Jamie:** Thanks for driving us to the Little League World Series, Ms. Thompson!

**Ms. Thompson:** No problem, Jamie! I know how much basketball means to you and Kyle.

**Kyle:** Mom, please! You're embarrassing me! The Little League World Series is not basketball.

| Stop | Think | Write |
VOCABULARY

If the setting is the <u>interior</u> of Ms. Thompson's car, where does the scene take place?

_____

_____

_____

**Jamie:** The Topeka Twins are our favorite baseball team, and Kyle looks exactly like their star pitcher, Chase Conway! *(teasing Kyle)* Now if only you could throw like him.

**Kyle:** Too bad Chase is hurt. I'd love to see him play!

*(The car comes to a stop outside of a baseball stadium.)*

**Ms. Thompson:** I'd hate for you to come all the way here only to miss the game. Do you have your tickets?

**Kyle:** Of course we have our tickets! I'm going to leave my jacket in the car. Doesn't look like rain today.

*(Kyle puts his coat in the car and shuts the door.)*

**Jamie:** Come on, Chase. It's time for your big game!

## Stop | Think | Write

MAKE PREDICTIONS

**Will Chase be playing in the game today? Why or why not?**

_____

_____

_____

15

## SCENE II

*(Moments later, Jamie and Kyle approach the Ticket Taker.)*

**Ticket Taker:** Tickets, please.

**Kyle:** Jamie, give him our tickets.

**Jamie:** *(looking at Kyle in surprise)* I thought you said you would hang on to them.

**Kyle:** Oh, no. I left them in my rain jacket! In the car!

**Ticket Taker:** Sorry, boys. I can't let you in. The game is sold out.

*(Jamie and Kyle step out of line, dejected.)*

**Kyle:** I'm so sorry, Jamie. I can't believe I **bungled** holding the tickets.

**Jamie:** Let's see if someone has an extra ticket.

**Stop** | **Think** | **Write**

VOCABULARY

How did Kyle **bungle** holding the tickets?

_____

_____

_____

16

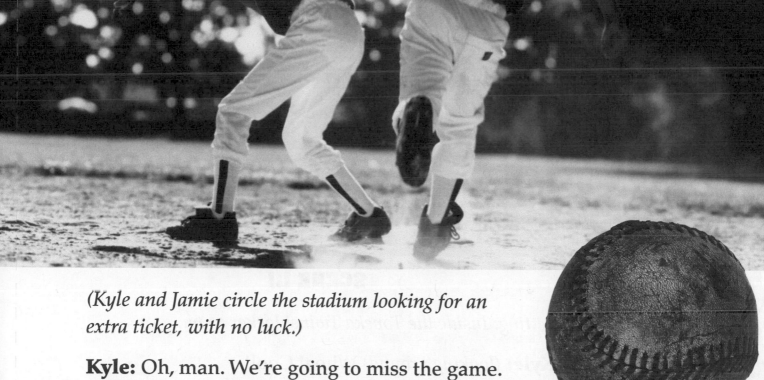

*(Kyle and Jamie circle the stadium looking for an extra ticket, with no luck.)*

**Kyle:** Oh, man. We're going to miss the game.

*(The Topeka Twins Manager appears from inside the stadium and waves to Kyle.)*

**Manager:** Chase! Over here!

**Jamie:** Huh? He's not . . . *(Kyle covers Jamie's mouth and turns him around.)*

**Kyle:** He thinks I'm Chase Conway! If I pretend to be Chase, I could get us into the game!

**Jamie:** But that's a lie. And you can't throw like Chase.

**Kyle:** I wouldn't have to throw like Chase. He's injured, remember? Just follow my lead. *(to the Manager)* Yeah, it's me, Chase! I'm coming!

## Stop | Think | Write

THEME

**Jamie seems worried about Kyle's plan. Why might he be worried?**

_____

_____

_____

17

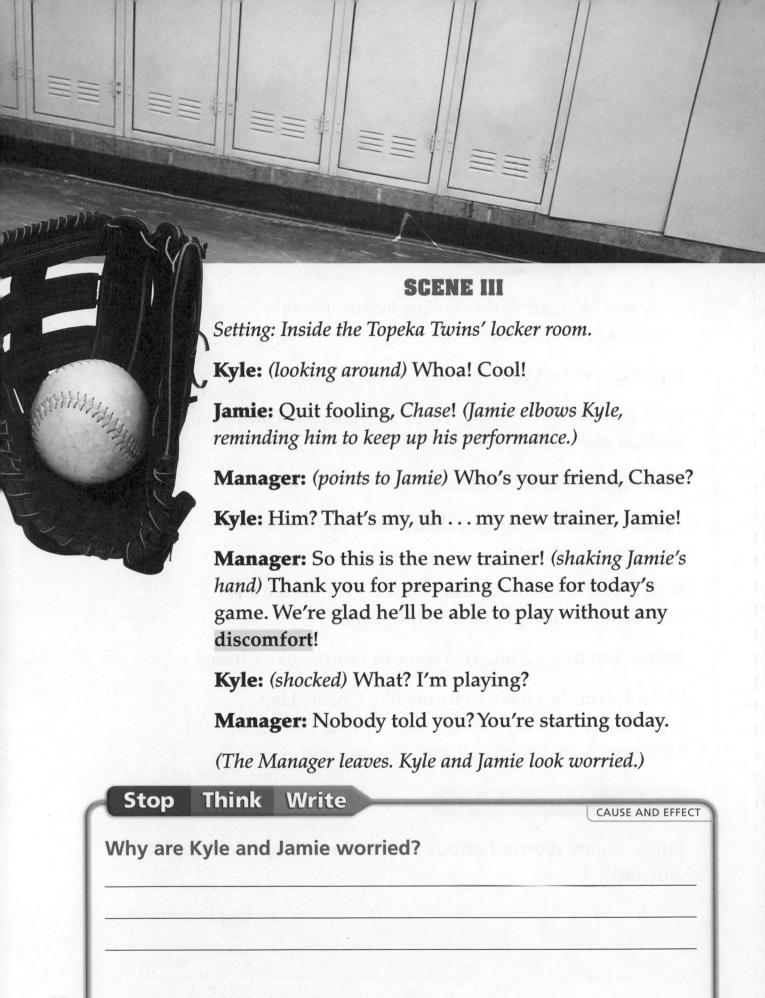

## SCENE III

*Setting: Inside the Topeka Twins' locker room.*

**Kyle:** *(looking around)* Whoa! Cool!

**Jamie:** Quit fooling, *Chase!* *(Jamie elbows Kyle, reminding him to keep up his performance.)*

**Manager:** *(points to Jamie)* Who's your friend, Chase?

**Kyle:** Him? That's my, uh . . . my new trainer, Jamie!

**Manager:** So this is the new trainer! *(shaking Jamie's hand)* Thank you for preparing Chase for today's game. We're glad he'll be able to play without any **discomfort!**

**Kyle:** *(shocked)* What? I'm playing?

**Manager:** Nobody told you? You're starting today.

*(The Manager leaves. Kyle and Jamie look worried.)*

**Stop** **Think** **Write**

CAUSE AND EFFECT

**Why are Kyle and Jamie worried?**

_____

_____

_____

18

**Kyle:** Jamie, I can't play like Chase.

**Jamie:** I guess you'll have to just tell him the truth.

**Kyle:** But I've already lied. And then we won't be able to see the game.

*(The Manager returns.)*

**Manager:** Okay, Chase, ready to go?

**Kyle:** Uh, sir, I'm not Chase Conway.

**Manager:** Come on, Chase. Stop playing around.

**Kyle:** No, I'm really not Chase. I just look like him.

**Manager:** What? You're not Chase? Who are you?

**Kyle:** We figured if you thought I was Chase, you'd let us into the game.

## Stop | Think | Write

**Where does Scene III take place?**

_____

_____

_____

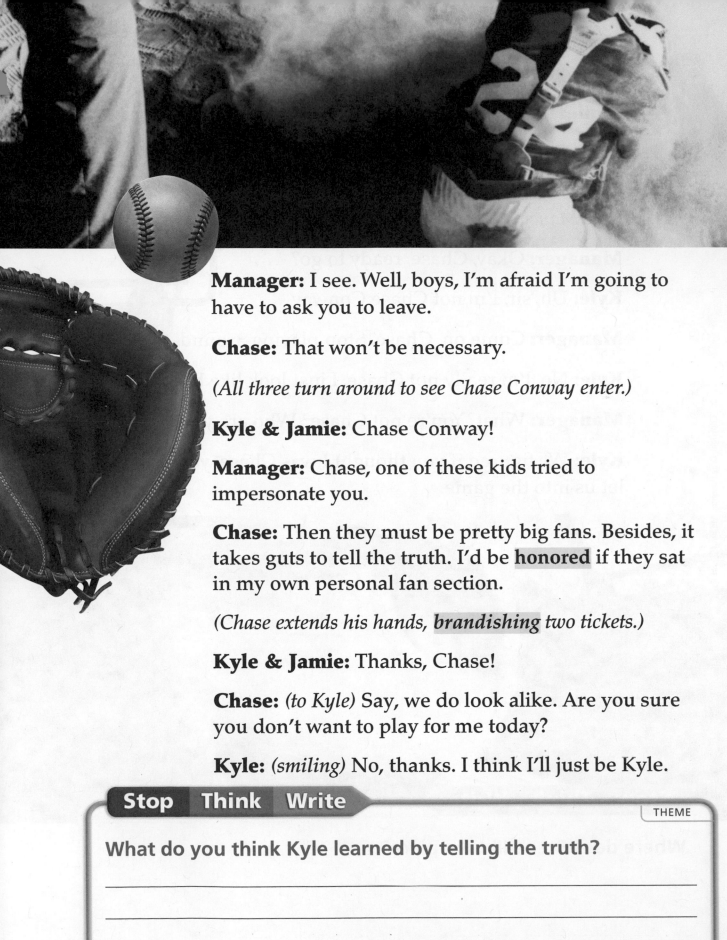

**Manager:** I see. Well, boys, I'm afraid I'm going to have to ask you to leave.

**Chase:** That won't be necessary.

*(All three turn around to see Chase Conway enter.)*

**Kyle & Jamie:** Chase Conway!

**Manager:** Chase, one of these kids tried to impersonate you.

**Chase:** Then they must be pretty big fans. Besides, it takes guts to tell the truth. I'd be honored if they sat in my own personal fan section.

*(Chase extends his hands, brandishing two tickets.)*

**Kyle & Jamie:** Thanks, Chase!

**Chase:** *(to Kyle)* Say, we do look alike. Are you sure you don't want to play for me today?

**Kyle:** *(smiling)* No, thanks. I think I'll just be Kyle.

| Stop | Think | Write |
| --- | --- | --- |

THEME

**What do you think Kyle learned by telling the truth?**

_____

_____

_____

## Look Back and Respond

**1** **How does Ms. Thompson embarrass Kyle?**

_____

_____

_____

**Hint**

For a clue, see page 14.

**2** **What is the setting for Scene II?**

_____

_____

_____

**Hint**

For a clue, see page 16.

**3** **How do Kyle and Jamie feel after the Manager tells Kyle he'll be playing in the big game?**

_____

_____

_____

_____

**Hint**

For clues, see pages 18 and 19.

**4** **What does Kyle learn by revealing to the Manager that he is not Chase?**

_____

_____

_____

_____

**Hint**

For a clue, see page 20.

# Be a Reading Detective!

Return to **A Royal Mystery**

"A Royal Mystery"
Student Book pp. 49–61

**1** What is one lesson about life that you can learn from the play?

☐ Teamwork is the key to success.

☐ People who are shy try harder.

☐ People with royal backgrounds will succeed.

**Prove It!** What evidence in the play supports your answer? Check the boxes. ☑ Make notes.

| Evidence | Notes |
|---|---|
| ☐ details about each girl's strengths | |
| ☐ how the girls become successful | |
| ☐ | |

### Write About It!

THEME

Answer question **1** using evidence from the text.

_____

_____

_____

_____

_____

_____

_____

**21A**

**2** At the end of the play, we learn that Rena is a princess. What clues in the play help readers guess this ending?

☐ how Rena looks in the illustrations

☐ how Rena acts and speaks

☐ other _____

**Prove It!** What evidence in the play supports your answer? Check the boxes. ☑ Make notes.

| Evidence | Notes |
|---|---|
| ☐ illustrations of Rena | |
| ☐ details about Rena's belongings | |
| ☐ the picture on page 59 | |

**Write About It!**

TEXT AND GRAPHIC FEATURES

Answer question **2** using evidence from the text.

_____

_____

_____

_____

_____

_____

_____

## Lesson 3

✓ **TARGET VOCABULARY**

**beckoned**
**debate**
**hesitated**
**scanned**
**shaken**

# A School Election

Joan and I were running for student council president. Before the election, we had an assembly. Joan and I had to answer questions because it was a

**1** _____.

When students asked questions, I answered each one quickly and well. I never **2** _____.

22

I **3** _____ the crowd of students, looking for friendly faces. It seemed to me that most people were on my side. I would certainly win the election.

The next day, the principal saw Joan and me in the hall. She **4** _____ to us. "I have the results of the election," she said.

"Joan, you won!" the principal said. What a shock! I couldn't believe that I wouldn't be president. I was **5** _____ by the principal's words.

# Tomás Decides

**by Duncan Searl**

"Sit down! Eat!" Mrs. Guzman urged. Before he sat down, Mr. Guzman cleared his throat to speak. "I just want to say how proud I am that Tomás is running for president of the student council."

Poor Tomás squirmed in his seat. Why did his father have to make such a big deal about that?

"My son will be a leader," Mr. Guzman said, "and he will change things for the better!"

Tomás **hesitated** for a moment. "Thanks, Papa," he said, "but my plans are, um, changing. When my friends asked me to run for student council, I agreed. Now I, er, I want to play baseball."

---

**Stop** **Think** **Write**

COMPARE AND CONTRAST

How do the plans of the father and the son differ?

_____

_____

_____

Mr. Guzman's face fell. He seemed **shaken** by the news. "Play baseball?" he repeated with a sad smile.

Tomás pressed his case. "That's right. The Raiders have a chance to win the championship," he said. "To do it, the team needs me there, a hundred percent!"

"Can't you do both, Tomás?" Mrs. Guzman asked.

"Not really, Mama. To win the student council seat, I have to give two speeches and take part in a **debate**. I have to make posters and talk to people. That all happens after school. So I'd miss practice sometimes, maybe even games. Besides, the student council never does anything important."

## Stop Think Write

VOCABULARY

**Why is Mr. Guzman <u>shaken</u> by what Tomás says?**

_____

_____

_____

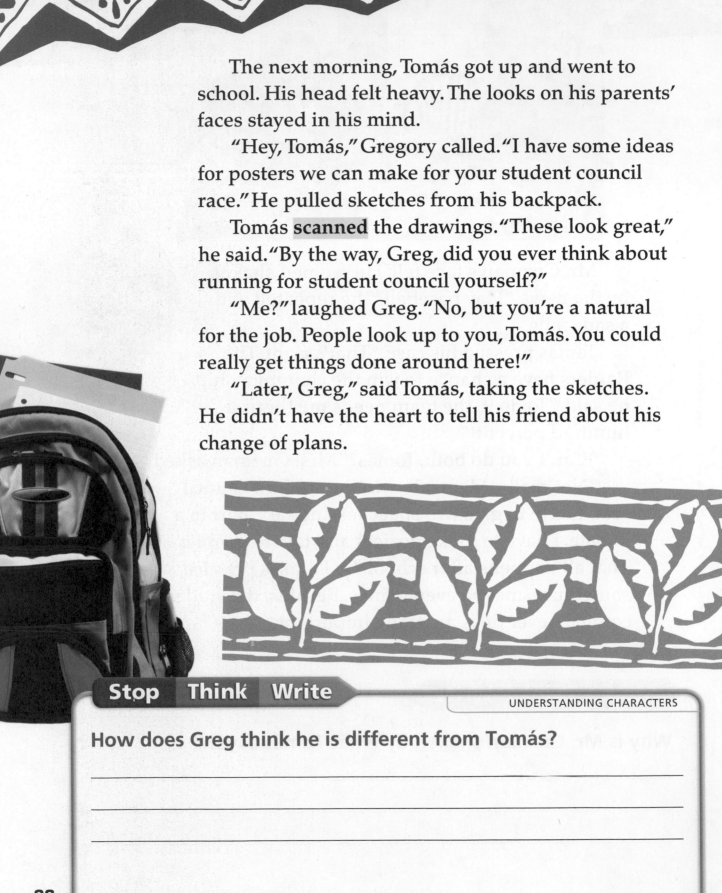

The next morning, Tomás got up and went to school. His head felt heavy. The looks on his parents' faces stayed in his mind.

"Hey, Tomás," Gregory called. "I have some ideas for posters we can make for your student council race." He pulled sketches from his backpack.

Tomás **scanned** the drawings. "These look great," he said. "By the way, Greg, did you ever think about running for student council yourself?"

"Me?" laughed Greg. "No, but you're a natural for the job. People look up to you, Tomás. You could really get things done around here!"

"Later, Greg," said Tomás, taking the sketches. He didn't have the heart to tell his friend about his change of plans.

## Stop | Think | Write

UNDERSTANDING CHARACTERS

**How does Greg think he is different from Tomás?**

_____

_____

_____

That afternoon, Tomás's class walked to Golden Greens. The class had already been to the senior citizen home twice. The students went there to talk with the seniors, play games, and learn firsthand about the past.

In the rec room, a tall, skinny man **beckoned** to Tomás. "Hey, Mr. Guzman! Come on over here and sit awhile." It was Mr. Jeffers, a man Tomás had played checkers with last time.

"Hello, Mr. Jeffers," Tomás said.

Mr. Jeffers smiled. "Call me Fastball."

"Why Fastball?" Tomás asked.

"Well, you know I can't walk anymore, but back in the day, I was a fastball pitcher."

"A major leaguer?" Tomás asked hopefully.

**Stop    Think    Write**

VOCABULARY

**Why do you think Mr. Jeffers beckoned to Tomás?**

_____

_____

_____

Mr. Jeffers smiled. "In the 1930s and 1940s, the Negro Leagues were as major a league as any black man could get into. Even so, I struck out batters with the best of them!"

Tomás had never heard of the Negro Leagues. So Mr. Jeffers showed him a photograph.

"In my day," Mr. Jeffers said, "blacks and whites couldn't play on the same teams. That wasn't right, and it wasn't fair, but that's the way it was."

"That's all changed now," said Tomás.

"Sure has," Mr. Jeffers agreed, "but only because some people cared enough to change it. A few good people changed the rules and the laws, and things got better."

Tomás didn't reply. He was thinking hard.

**Stop Think Write**

**How did major league baseball change after the 1940s?**

_____

_____

_____

Mr. Jeffers broke the silence. "Are you a ballplayer, Tomás?"

"Shortstop. Our team could win the championship."

"Looking forward to that, are you?"

Tomás blurted out his feelings. He told Mr. Jeffers about his dilemma.

"Winning ballgames is good," Mr. Jeffers said. "However, improving a situation can make all the difference. I know from experience."

"Thanks, Fastball," Tomás said. "I guess I'll have to decide."

## Stop | Think | Write

UNDERSTANDING CHARACTERS

**Why isn't Tomás sure about playing baseball?**

_____

_____

_____

Walking back to school, Tomás caught up with Greg. "I've been thinking more about your sketches," Tomás said. "Will you help me make the posters?"

"Sure," said Greg. "By the way, do you have any ideas for the speech you have to make?"

"We all know our school could be a lot better," said Tomás. "Let's get our friends together after school for a meeting. I want everyone to make some suggestions. We need to choose the ideas that will really make a difference!"

"Don't you have baseball practice?"

"I can go to practice tomorrow," Tomás said. "This is important after all."

## Stop · Think · Write

COMPARE AND CONTRAST

**How have Tomás's feelings changed?**

_____

_____

_____

# Look Back and Respond

**1** **What decision does Tomás have to make?**

_____

_____

_____

**Hint**

See pages 24 and 25.

**2** **How does Mr. Jeffers help Tomás make his decision?**

_____

_____

_____

**Hint**

For a clue, see page 28.

**3** **How does Tomás change during this story?**

_____

_____

_____

**Hint**

For clues, see pages 24 and 30.

**4** **Do you think Tomás makes the right decision? Why?**

_____

_____

_____

**Hint**

Your answers to questions 2 and 3 should help you.

# Be a Reading Detective!

Return to

"Off and Running"
Student Book pp. 85–97

**1** **What is the main difference between Miata's ideas and Rudy's ideas?**

☐ Miata's ideas appeal to girls; Rudy's appeal to boys.

☐ Miata's ideas are useful; Rudy's are fun.

☐ Miata has one idea; Rudy has several.

**Prove It!** What evidence in the story supports your answer? Check the boxes. ☑ Make notes.

| Evidence | Notes |
|---|---|
| ☐ Miata's ideas | |
| ☐ Rudy's ideas | |
| ☐ how students react to the ideas | |
| ☐ | |

## Write About It!

COMPARE AND CONTRAST

Answer question **1** using evidence from the text.

_____

_____

_____

_____

_____

_____

_____

**2** **Which sentence best describes Miata's father?**

☐ He is very competitive and wants Miata to win.

☐ He works hard and is very serious.

☐ He wants Miata to do good things, whether she wins or not.

☐ other _____

**Prove It!** What evidence in the story supports your answer?
Check the boxes. ☑ Make notes.

| Evidence | Notes |
|---|---|
| ☐ what Miata says and does | |
| ☐ what Miata's father says and does | |
| ☐ | |

**Write About It!**

UNDERSTANDING CHARACTERS

Answer question **2** using evidence from the text.

_____

_____

_____

_____

_____

_____

_____

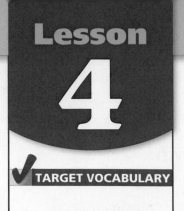

## Lesson 4

✓ **TARGET VOCABULARY**

**competition**
**element**
**intimidated**
**mastered**
**routine**

# Teamwork

**1** When you first join a team, you probably won't be the best at everything. Don't be **intimidated** by teammates who have been there longer. They had to start out just like you.

**What other situations could make a person feel <u>intimidated</u>?**

_____

_____

_____

**2** Remember, you're not in a **competition** with your teammates. You all work together to make the team as good as it can be.

**Name a <u>competition</u> that you have been in.**

_____

_____

_____

**3** As a team, you'll probably work out a **routine** together. If you're on a sports team, you'll practice at a set time each week. If you're in a singing group, you'll work on the ways you perform your songs.

**What <u>routine</u> do you have in the morning before you go to school?**

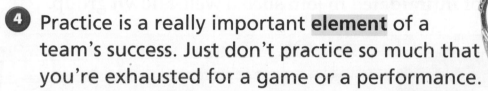

**4** Practice is a really important **element** of a team's success. Just don't practice so much that you're exhausted for a game or a performance.

**What is another <u>element</u> of a team's success?**

**5** Once you've **mastered** your skills, you'll truly be part of the team!

**What skills has an acrobat <u>mastered</u>?**

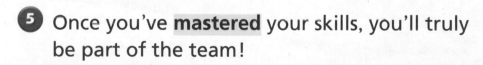

# The All-Wrong All-Stars

## by Selena Rodo

"You can't convince me to do it," I said to my mom, gazing out the window to hide my feelings.

"Selena, you sing so well. I'd be sad to see you waste your talent," she said.

"So you like my crowing?" I said, frowning.

"You sing!" Mom was quick to respond. "You do *not* crow. Honey, just think about it before you say no."

"I'll sleep on it," I said. The truth is, I felt kind of **intimidated** to join such a well-known group.

**Stop** | **Think** | **Write**

Write a synonym for the word <u>intimidated</u>.

_____

The All-City Glee Club was the best showcase around for singers. They were all male, but now females could be a part of the group. Yesterday, Mr. Willow asked Inez, Yolanda, and me to join. He said he wanted female voices as an **element** of the show.

At first, I said no. I didn't think their style would suit me. The All-City Glee Club tends to sing low notes with a slow beat. My talent was singing high notes with a fast beat. I didn't think my singing would fit in with theirs at all. Also, there were bound to be some fans who wouldn't be happy to see girls in the group.

**Stop** | **Think** | **Write**

INFER AND PREDICT

**Why might some fans be unhappy to see girls in the group?**

_____

_____

_____

The next morning, I looked out my window. The last snow of the winter had melted. Small green buds had started to grow on the trees. Maybe it was time for me to grow, too!

"Mom, I'm going to sing with All-City," I said. "I think that I need to at least give it a try."

My mom was all smiles. "Good for you, Selena. I know you can do this."

Later, in class, Mr. Willow explained that the All-City Glee Club would now be called the All-City All-Stars. We were thrilled to be a part of this new group.

## Stop | Think | Write

CAUSE AND EFFECT

**What makes the author decide to give singing with the All-City Glee Club a try?**

_____

_____

_____

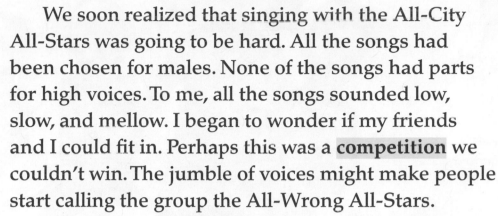

We soon realized that singing with the All-City All-Stars was going to be hard. All the songs had been chosen for males. None of the songs had parts for high voices. To me, all the songs sounded low, slow, and mellow. I began to wonder if my friends and I could fit in. Perhaps this was a **competition** we couldn't win. The jumble of voices might make people start calling the group the All-Wrong All-Stars.

"I think this is a mistake," I said to Dad after school. "There are no parts in their songs for our high voices. When all of us sing together, it sounds terrible!"

"Don't give up, Selena," Dad declared. "Find a way to show what you can do."

## Stop | Think | Write

CAUSE AND EFFECT

**Why does the author tell her dad she thinks joining the group was a mistake?**

_____

_____

_____

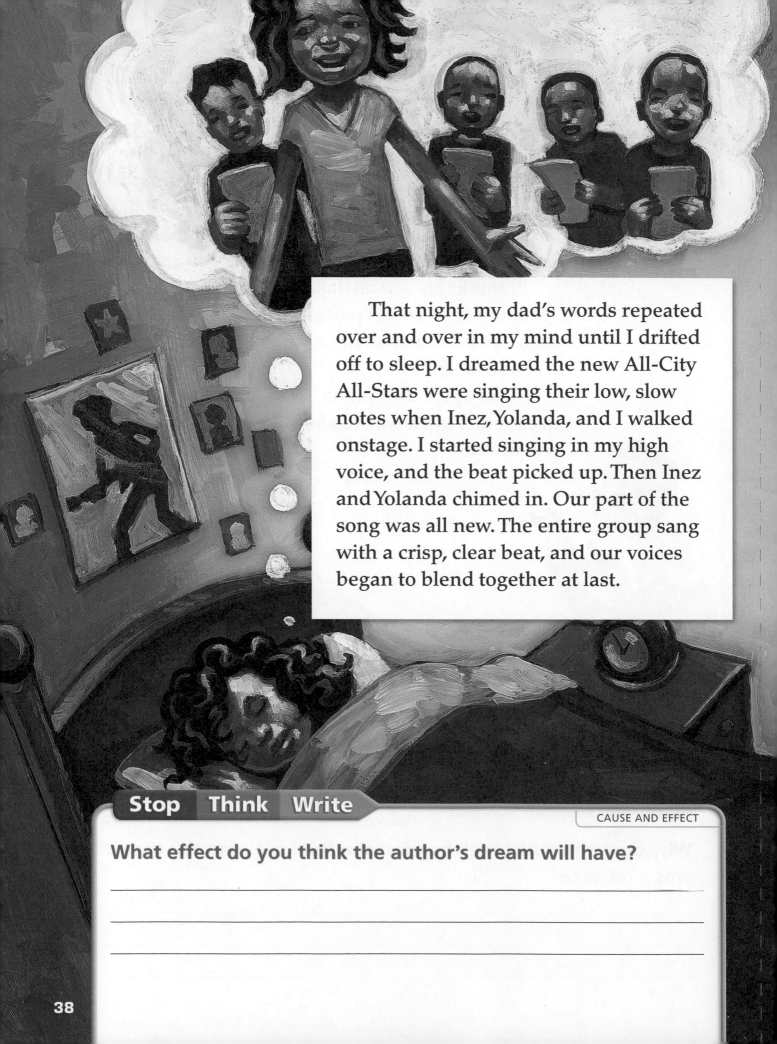

That night, my dad's words repeated over and over in my mind until I drifted off to sleep. I dreamed the new All-City All-Stars were singing their low, slow notes when Inez, Yolanda, and I walked onstage. I started singing in my high voice, and the beat picked up. Then Inez and Yolanda chimed in. Our part of the song was all new. The entire group sang with a crisp, clear beat, and our voices began to blend together at last.

## Stop | Think | Write

CAUSE AND EFFECT

**What effect do you think the author's dream will have?**

_____

_____

_____

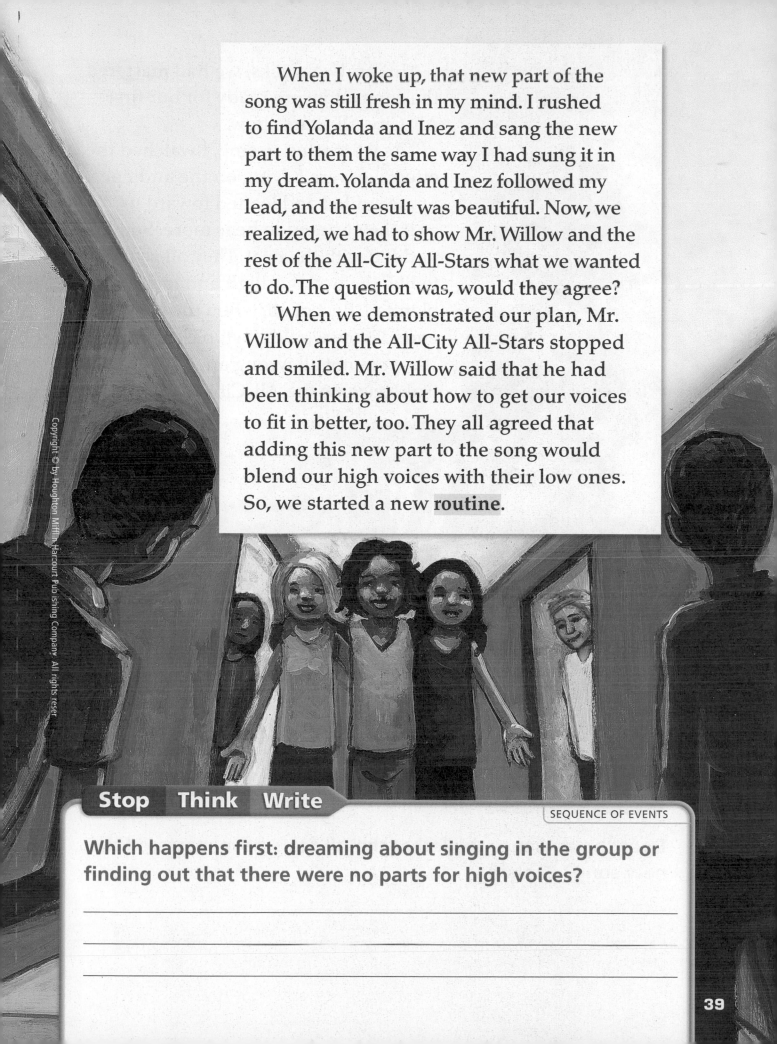

When I woke up, that new part of the song was still fresh in my mind. I rushed to find Yolanda and Inez and sang the new part to them the same way I had sung it in my dream. Yolanda and Inez followed my lead, and the result was beautiful. Now, we realized, we had to show Mr. Willow and the rest of the All-City All-Stars what we wanted to do. The question was, would they agree?

When we demonstrated our plan, Mr. Willow and the All-City All-Stars stopped and smiled. Mr. Willow said that he had been thinking about how to get our voices to fit in better, too. They all agreed that adding this new part to the song would blend our high voices with their low ones. So, we started a new routine.

**Stop** | **Think** | **Write**

SEQUENCE OF EVENTS

**Which happens first: dreaming about singing in the group or finding out that there were no parts for high voices?**

_____

_____

_____

In just two weeks, we had **mastered** the song and were ready for our first All-City All-Stars show.

As we started to sing, I watched the effect we were having on the audience. Some smiled and leaned toward us, as if they wanted to hear more. Some nodded with the beat. They all seemed to like the way our high and low voices blended. Best of all, when the song ended, they wouldn't stop clapping. We were not all wrong after all! We had truly become the All-City All-Stars.

**Stop | Think | Write**

Does the audience think that the All-Stars have <u>mastered</u> the new song? Explain.

_____

_____

_____

# Look Back and Respond

**1** How does the author's mother feel about her joining the All-City Glee Club?

**Hint**

For clues, look on page 34.

_____

_____

_____

**2** At first, what makes it so difficult for the girls to sing with the group?

**Hint**

For a clue, see page 37.

_____

_____

_____

**3** Is the advice the author's father gives her good or bad? Explain.

**Hint**

See page 37 and the following pages.

_____

_____

_____

**4** How do the author's feelings about joining the singing group change through the story?

**Hint**

Look for clues throughout the story, especially on the last page.

_____

_____

_____

# Be a Reading Detective!

**Return to**

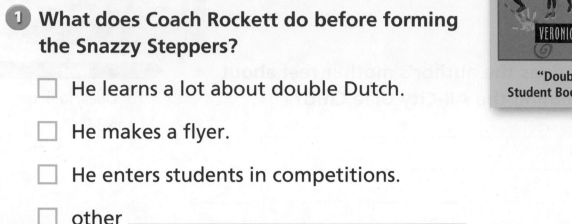

"Double Dutch"
Student Book pp. 115–125

**1** **What does Coach Rockett do before forming the Snazzy Steppers?**

☐ He learns a lot about double Dutch.

☐ He makes a flyer.

☐ He enters students in competitions.

☐ other _____

## Prove It! What evidence in the selection supports your answer? Check the boxes. ☑ Make notes.

| Evidence | Notes |
|---|---|
| ☐ details about the Snazzy Steppers | |
| ☐ details about Coach Rockett | |
| ☐ | |

## Write About It!

SEQUENCE OF EVENTS

**Answer question 1 using evidence from the text.**

_____

_____

_____

_____

_____

_____

_____

**2** What is the most important lesson about life that readers can learn from the selection?

☐ Activities that students already enjoy are meaningful.

☐ You can succeed even if you start from scratch.

☐ The key to success in double Dutch is rhythm.

**Prove It!** What evidence in the selection supports your answer? Check the boxes. ☑ Make notes.

| Evidence | Notes |
|---|---|
| ☐ the coach's experience with double Dutch | |
| ☐ the students' experience with double Dutch | |
| ☐ | |

**Write About It!**

THEME

Answer question **2** using evidence from the text.

_____

_____

_____

_____

_____

_____

_____

## Working with a Partner

**embarrassed
gorgeous
obvious
preliminary
typically**

**Check the answer.**

**1** At my school, students _____ work in pairs to complete a project.

☐ **gradually** ☐ **acutely** ☐ **typically**

**2** It's helpful to have a partner present your work if you are _____ to speak in public.

☐ **delicate** ☐ **embarrassed** ☐ **obvious**

**3** It is _____ that two people will come up with more ideas than one person.

☐ **acute** ☐ **obvious** ☐ **gorgeous**

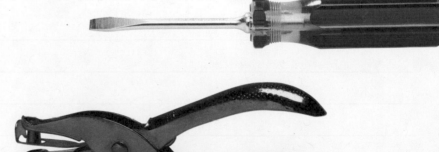

**4** Partners can come up with _____ plans on their own and then work together on the final plan.

☐ **preliminary**　☐ **inflated**　☐ **embarrassed**

**5** When two talented students work together, the artwork that they produce can be _____.

☐ **embarrassed**　☐ **tethered**　☐ **gorgeous**

**6** How would you help someone who was <u>embarrassed</u> to speak in front of the class?

_____

_____

_____

**7** Describe a painting or photograph that you think is <u>gorgeous</u>.

_____

_____

_____

**8** What do you <u>typically</u> do before you go to school?

_____

_____

# It Takes Teamwork

## by Mia Lewis

Sitting at her desk, Carla scanned the line of classmates as they filed in to take their seats.

"What happened to you?" she asked a dripping Ben as he shuffled into class. His soaked sneakers squeaked as he passed by.

"I was waiting at the bus stop when this huge truck came down the hill and splashed me!" he said.

"Looks like you and the truck started the day on a downhill slope," Carla joked.

### Stop · Think · Write

CONCLUSIONS AND GENERALIZATIONS

**How can you tell that Carla and Ben are friends?**

_____

_____

_____

44

"This is Teamwork Week," said Ms. Kim. "You will team up with a classmate to make a model of some kind."

Carla decided she would ask Ben. They would make a good team.

"**Typically**, I let you pick your own partners," explained Ms. Kim. "This time I am going to pull two names at a time from a box. The names I pick will be teammates."

Carla sat completely still as Ms. Kim called out the names.

"Carla Vargas and, let's see, Wendell Oaks."

"Oh, no," Carla said to herself. "I don't know him."

---

**Stop** **Think** **Write**

VOCABULARY

**What would typically happen if Carla and Ben wanted to work together?**

_____

_____

_____

Carla agreed to meet Wendell after school to work on the project.

Later, at Wendell's home, Mrs. Oaks greeted Carla and invited her to come inside. "Wendell is down in his lab," she explained.

"Lab? Just what am I getting into now?" Carla wondered as she stepped down the stairs.

In the basement, Wendell had just finished working on a model car.

"Do you like making models?" Carla asked.

"I sure do," Wendell said. "Do you?"

**Stop** | **Think** | **Write**

THEME

Carla seems worried about working with someone she doesn't know. Why might that be a problem?

_____

_____

_____

46

"I'm no good at it," Carla said. She was **embarrassed** to tell about the model boat she made last year. It had floated for only a few seconds.

"Well, it takes two to make a team," said Wendell. "I'm sure you have a talent to add."

"I *am* good at coming up with ideas and making plans," offered Carla. "What if we make a model for an amusement park ride?"

"Yes!" Wendell agreed. "Let's make it a floating boat ride."

"Um, sure," said Carla, sounding very uncertain.

## Stop · Think · Write

UNDERSTANDING CHARACTERS

What skills does Carla have that she can contribute to the team?

_____

_____

_____

Carla made a **preliminary** sketch before they began to build. Wendell looked for materials. It was **obvious** that Wendell knew what he was doing! Carla was amazed at the hanging vines he made out of clay. Carla made a cave for the boat ride.

The teammates put the model in a pan filled with water. The water was a lake around the island. They made small boats from small trays. The trays had little foam balls underneath to help keep them afloat. Wendell linked the boats with string.

### Stop · Think · Write

What makes it <u>obvious</u> that Wendell knows how to make models?

_____

_____

_____

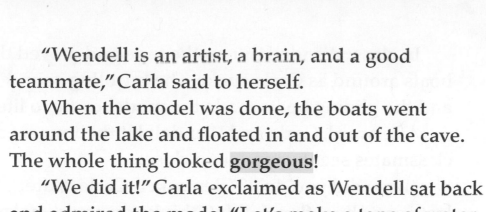

"Wendell is an artist, a brain, and a good teammate," Carla said to herself.

When the model was done, the boats went around the lake and floated in and out of the cave. The whole thing looked **gorgeous**!

"We did it!" Carla exclaimed as Wendell sat back and admired the model. "Let's make a tape of water burbling, like in a stream," she said. "We can play it while we give our presentation."

"Good plan!" agreed Wendell, reaching for a tape recorder.

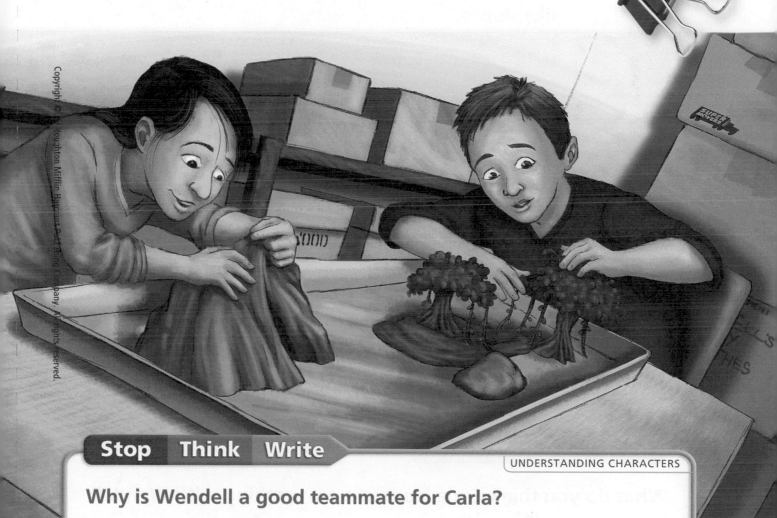

## Stop | Think | Write

**Why is Wendell a good teammate for Carla?**

_____

_____

_____

In class, Wendell put on the tape and moved the boats around as Carla spoke. The burbling sound and the gliding boats made the model come to life.

Afterward, Carla and Wendell let their amazed classmates see the model up close.

"How did you do it?" Ben asked Carla. "After last year's boat flop, I didn't think you could make a thing!"

"Carla planned it all," Wendell boasted.

"Well, Wendell made the plan work," Carla insisted. "Without him, the boats would have sunk like stones."

**Stop** | **Think** | **Write**

What do you think Carla learned from working with Wendell on the project?

_____

_____

_____

# Look Back and Respond

**1** How does Carla feel about working with Wendell at first?

_____

_____

_____

**Hint**

For clues, see pages 45 and 46.

**2** What does Wendell contribute to the project?

_____

_____

_____

**Hint**

Look for clues on pages 48 and 49.

**3** What does Carla learn about Wendell through her teamwork with him?

_____

_____

_____

**Hint**

For a clue, see page 49.

**4** Do you think "Teamwork Week" was a success for Carla and Wendell? Explain your answer.

_____

_____

_____

**Hint**

You can find clues throughout the story.

# Be a Reading Detective!

Return to

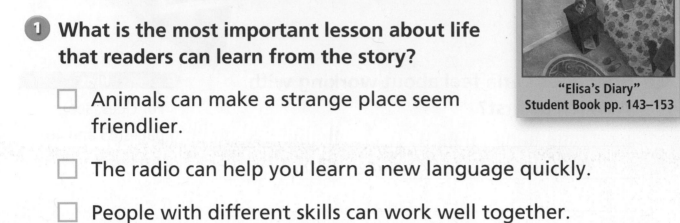

"Elisa's Diary"
Student Book pp. 143–153

**1** **What is the most important lesson about life that readers can learn from the story?**

☐ Animals can make a strange place seem friendlier.

☐ The radio can help you learn a new language quickly.

☐ People with different skills can work well together.

**Prove It!** What evidence in the story supports your answer?
Check the boxes. ☑ Make notes.

| Evidence | Notes |
|---|---|
| ☐ when Elisa and José become friends | |
| ☐ what Elisa says to her class at the end | |
| ☐ | |

**Write About It!**

THEME

Answer question **1** using evidence from the text.

_____

_____

_____

_____

_____

_____

_____

**2** How are Elisa and José similar?

☐ They both have trouble expressing themselves in English.

☐ They both learn English by listening to people speak it.

☐ other _____

**Prove It!** What evidence in the story supports your answer?
Check the boxes. ☑ Make notes.

| Evidence | Notes |
|---|---|
| ☐ events in school | |
| ☐ events outside school | |
| ☐ | |

**Write About It!**

COMPARE AND CONTRAST

Answer question **2** using evidence from the text.

_____

_____

_____

_____

_____

_____

_____

**Lesson**

# 6

✓ **TARGET VOCABULARY**

dwarfed
perch
presence
procedure
transferred

# MAKE ROOM FOR MONKEYS

Around the world there are about 200

different kinds of monkeys. Some monkeys live

in trees, but others live on the ground. Some

species, such as tamarins, are small. These species

are **1** _____ by their larger

monkey cousins, such as baboons.

Monkeys that live in trees can

**2** _____ on branches

above the ground. All monkeys can hold

onto branches with their hands and feet.

Some monkeys can swing by their tails.

Human activity threatens the ongoing

**3** _____ of some monkeys

in the wild. For example, brown spider monkeys

are critically endangered. Proboscis monkeys are

endangered. Being critically endangered means

that someday soon there may not be any left at all

on Earth.

Some endangered monkeys have been

**4** _____ from the

wild to new homes in zoos. This

**5** _____ may help

monkeys survive. However, the best hope

for endangered monkeys is that their

homes in the wild be saved. If people want to

share the Earth with animals, we have to choose

carefully what we do with land.

# WILL THE AMERICAN CHESTNUT SURVIVE?

## by Dina McClellan

*Under a spreading chestnut tree*
*The village smithy stands;*
*The smith, a mighty man is he,*
*With large and sinewy hands . . .*

**—from "The Village Blacksmith" by**
**Henry Wadsworth Longfellow (1807–1882)**

## A CELEBRATED TREE

The American chestnut tree was one of the most celebrated forest trees in the northeastern United States. It once grew across millions of acres from Maine to Mississippi. At 110 feet tall, these trees **dwarfed** all others. The Appalachians were so thickly covered with them that when they flowered, the mountaintops turned white. In the fall, the earth was black with fallen chestnuts.

---

**Stop** **Think** **Write**

AUTHOR'S PURPOSE

Why do you think the author introduced this article with these lines from a famous poem?

_____

_____

_____

# A MYSTERIOUS FUNGUS

Today, the **presence** of the American chestnut in the region has been reduced to almost nothing. The reason is a mysterious fungus. It was first discovered in 1904 at the Bronx Zoo in New York City. Within two years, all the chestnut trees at the zoo were dead or dying. In another fifty years, the fungus would kill four billion trees across the eastern United States.

This is a fungus that spreads easily. Puffs of spores (tiny, seed-like particles that can grow into a fungus) fly through the air and are **transferred** to the fur and feathers of animals. When these animals **perch** on chestnut trees, the spores can settle in the cracks in the bark. The fungus grows around the tree and strangles it.

**Stop** **Think** **Write**

CAUSE AND EFFECT

How do the killer spores get into the tree trunk?

_____

_____

_____

But all is not lost. The American chestnut has two things going for it: (1) the fungus can't kill the roots, and (2) the roots can grow into new trees. That's the good news. The bad news is that the fungus still lives in the region and can attack new chestnut growth.

Stop | Think | Write

CONCLUSIONS

**Why might the American chestnut become extinct one day?**

_____

_____

_____

# HUMANS TO THE RESCUE

In the 1930s, scientists thought the American chestnut could be saved. They discovered the Chinese chestnut, a relative of the American tree. The big difference was that the Chinese chestnut came from the same region as the fungus, so it had a kind of built-in protection. The Chinese chestnut could not get sick.

The scientists cross-bred the two species, hoping the result would be young trees that looked American but didn't get sick. It didn't work, however, and this work ended in the 1970s.

## Stop | Think | Write

PROBLEM AND SOLUTION

**Why did scientists of the 1930s believe that the Chinese chestnut could help solve the problem?**

_____

_____

_____

Then, in the 1980s, a scientist named Dr. Charles Burnham teamed up with a Minnesota chestnut farmer to find a new way of breeding the two trees.

First, the Chinese chestnut was crossed with the American chestnut, resulting in young trees that were half Chinese and half American. Then, these young trees were crossed back with the American parent, over and over again. The result of this **procedure** is an American tree that doesn't get sick.

**Stop** **Think** **Write**

How was Dr. Burnham's procedure different than the one used in the 1930s?

_____

_____

_____

# THE AMERICAN CHESTNUT FOUNDATION

In 1983, an organization called the American Chestnut Foundation was set up to support the program started by Dr. Burnham. Its members are hopeful that once the trees have been bred they can be put back into the forest using a process called reforestation. Then it's up to nature to keep things going.

## Stop | Think | Write

MAIN IDEA AND DETAILS

What do the members of the American Chestnut Foundation want to do with the new trees they have bred?

_____

_____

_____

Hundreds of trees have been reforested in Virginia and Tennessee, and they appear to be doing well. But more time is needed to know if the trees can survive in the long run. Reforestation is a huge task that takes many years of hard work.

Foundation members truly care about these proud and beautiful trees. They believe that someday the famous "spreading chestnut tree" will regain its rightful place in the American forest.

**Stop** | **Think** | **Write**

MAIN IDEA AND DETAILS

**Why is the survival of the American chestnut still uncertain?**

_____

_____

_____

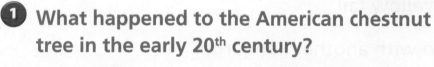

# Look Back and Respond

**1** **What happened to the American chestnut tree in the early 20th century?**

**Hint**

For clues, see pages 54 and 55.

_____

_____

_____

**2** **How does the fungus kill the trees?**

**Hint**

For a description, see page 55.

_____

_____

_____

**3** **What makes the Chinese chestnut such a good choice for cross-breeding?**

**Hint**

For clues, see page 57.

_____

_____

_____

**4** **What are the goals of the American Chestnut Foundation?**

**Hint**

For clues, see page 59.

_____

_____

_____

# Be a Reading Detective!

**Return to**

"Quest for the Tree Kangaroo"
Student Book pp. 175–189

**1** A tracker climbs a tree near where a tree kangaroo is sitting. What effect does this have on the kangaroo?

☐ She jumps to a lower tree and is captured.

☐ She has a long, yellow tail.

☐ She is discovered with another kangaroo.

**Prove It!** What evidence in the selection supports your answer? Check the boxes. ☑ Make notes.

| Evidence | Notes |
|---|---|
| ☐ events before the tracker climbs the tree | |
| ☐ events after he climbs the tree | |
| ☐ the photographs | |

**Write About It!**

CAUSE AND EFFECT

Answer question **1** using evidence from the text.

_____

_____

_____

_____

_____

_____

_____

**2** **One main idea is that the scientists study whatever they can about tree kangaroos.** Which details do the scientists study?

☐ the kangaroos' size, heart rate, breathing, and temperature

☐ the kangaroos' behavior in the wild

☐ other _____

**Prove It!** What evidence in the selection supports your answer? Check the boxes. ☑ Make notes.

| Evidence | Notes |
|---|---|
| ☐ how the scientists find the animals | |
| ☐ what they measure after they capture the animals | |
| ☐ | |

**Write About It!**

MAIN IDEAS AND DETAILS

Answer question **2** using evidence from the text.

_____

_____

_____

_____

_____

_____

# Alarm on the Farm

**bounding
frantic
lunging
picturing
romp**

The farmer got quite **frantic**
when he took a look outside.
The farmyard was a total mess,
and that's not all he spied.

The goat was **bounding** down the lane
and bleating with each stride.
A goose was sitting on its back,
quite pleased about the ride.

Three pigs were charging here and there.
The sheepdog joined the **romp**.
The cows looked on in horror
and forgot to even chomp.

The bull was **lunging** at the cat.
The cat leapt in the air.
It jumped in fright into the pond
and gave the ducks a scare.

The farmer called out to his wife
and ran toward the door.
He muttered something, **picturing**
the work he had in store.

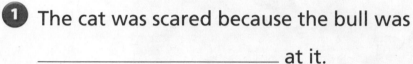

**1** The cat was scared because the bull was

_____ at it.

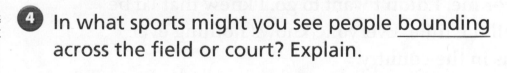

**2** The sheepdog and the three pigs had a

_____ in the farmyard.

**3** The sight of his farm in an uproar made the

farmer _____ .

**4** In what sports might you see people <u>bounding</u>
across the field or court? Explain.

_____

_____

_____

**5** If you were <u>picturing</u> your perfect spot, what
would it be like?

_____

_____

_____

# Nothing Ever Happens in the Country

## by Shawn Boyle

A few months ago, Mom and Dad told me that we would be moving to the country. They were tired of the **frantic** pace of city life. They wanted some peace and quiet. So, they had decided that we would live out in the middle of nowhere. On a farm!

As for me, I didn't want to go. I knew that I'd be bored all the time. Everyone knows nothing ever happens in the country.

I was right. It didn't take me very long to realize that I didn't like the country one bit.

## Stop | Think | Write

VOCABULARY

**How would life on a farm be different from the family's frantic city life?**

_____

_____

_____

Even my birthday on the farm was boring. In the city, I would have had all my friends over, and we would have had a great time. In the country, the only kid who came to my party was the goat! He tried to steal my birthday cake right off the picnic table.

Mom told me that I'd make lots of new friends when school started. I just shrugged my shoulders. Then Mom and Dad told me that they had a surprise for me. They had arranged for my best friend Kwan to come visit for a week. That was really great news.

**Stop** **Think** **Write**

CAUSE AND EFFECT

**Why does the narrator shrug his shoulders?**

_____

_____

_____

It was only a few days until Kwan would arrive, but it seemed like years. Mom kept telling me to go outside and enjoy the sunshine. Why would I? I didn't feel like sharing my meals with the goat. I didn't need to have a **romp** with the barnyard chickens.

As I listened to Mom, I kept reading my comic books and **picturing** life in the city. I missed the noise—the honking horns, the sirens, the loud buses.

**Stop** **Think** **Write**

UNDERSTANDING CHARACTERS

**What can you tell about the narrator from his thoughts about going outside?**

_____

_____

_____

Finally, Kwan arrived. Dad and I met him at the train station. I warned him that he could expect a really boring week, but he was really excited. He had never been to a farm before. On the ride home, he could not hide his enthusiasm. He pointed at a wild turkey on the side of the road, at a groundhog chewing grass, and even at a herd of cows.

Still, I was sure that Kwan would soon find out how boring life on a farm really was.

**Stop** **Think** **Write**

UNDERSTANDING CHARACTERS

**What do Kwan's reactions to the country tell you about him?**

_____

_____

_____

The next morning, Kwan was up at the crack of dawn. I watched him **bounding** over to the chicken coop, and then I followed him at a slower pace.

Kwan was thrilled to find a couple of eggs there. "Talk about fresh!" he said. "Boy, this is the life."

I wasn't sure that having eggs for breakfast was such an amazing event, but Kwan's good mood rubbed off on me. It didn't last very long, though. Kwan wanted to go for a hike. What could be duller than that? As he was my best friend, I pretended to be excited.

**Stop** **Think** **Write**

VOCABULARY

Why do you think Kwan was <u>bounding</u> over to the chicken coop?

_____

_____

_____

Mom had packed us lunch and had made sure we took binoculars with us. I couldn't imagine why we would need them. I didn't think it would take very long for Kwan to get bored, binoculars or no binoculars.

I was wrong. Everything Kwan saw amazed him. Birds, trees, grass, everything made him happy. Then he tugged at my sleeve and pointed up at the sky at some hawks circling. We both grabbed our binoculars. The birds were awesome! Suddenly, we saw one of the hawks **lunging** toward the ground. The next second, it flew back up with a tiny mouse in its claws. The hike wasn't so bad, after all.

**Stop   Think   Write**

CAUSE AND EFFECT

**What changes the narrator's feelings about the hike?**

_____

_____

_____

Our trip through the woods got even better. We saw a tree so filled with termites it was ready to fall down. We heard a hammering noise and looked up to see a woodpecker. In the next tree there was a beehive. A little later we saw a fox and some skunks. We didn't get too close to the skunks!

We were both exhausted when we got home. Before we went to bed, we talked about what we would do the next day, and the next. Slowly it dawned on me—living in the country was as exciting as I would let it be. It had taken a city boy to show me!

## Stop Think Write

INFER AND PREDICT

**Why don't Kwan and the narrator get too close to the skunks?**

_____

_____

_____

# Look Back and Respond

**1** Why is it important that the boys take binoculars on their hike?

_____

_____

_____

**Hint**

For a clue, see page 69.

**2** What animals are there on the farm?

_____

_____

_____

**Hint**

For clues, see pages 65 and 66.

**3** What can you tell about Kwan's character?

_____

_____

_____

**Hint**

For clues, see pages 67 through 70.

**4** How do the narrator and Kwan differ?

_____

_____

_____

**Hint**

Clues are on every page.

# Be a Reading Detective!

**1** **In which ways does Travis show that he loves Arliss?**

☐ He puts up with Arliss's behavior.

☐ He comes running when Arliss screams.

☐ He is prepared to fight the bear to save Arliss.

☐ other _____

**Prove It!** What evidence in the story supports your answer?
Check the boxes. ✓ Make notes.

| Evidence | Notes |
|---|---|
| ☐ events in the text | |
| ☐ what Travis thinks and feels | |
| ☐ | |

**Write About It!**

UNDERSTANDING CHARACTERS

Answer question **1** using evidence from the text.

_____

_____

_____

_____

_____

_____

_____

**2** Travis says that Old Yeller is a "meat-stealing rascal." How do his feelings about the dog change?

☐ He respects the way the dog fights.

☐ He realizes that the dog looks after the family.

☐ other _____

**Prove It!** What evidence in the story supports your answer? Check the boxes. ☑ Make notes.

| Evidence | Notes |
|---|---|
| ☐ what Old Yeller does | |
| ☐ what Travis thinks | |
| ☐ | |

**Write About It!**

COMPARE AND CONTRAST

Answer question **2** using evidence from the text.

_____
_____
_____
_____
_____
_____
_____

endangered
regulate
responsibility
restore
vegetation

# Oil Spills

**1** Big boats called tankers carry oil around the world. Oil companies own these tankers. Laws **regulate** the number of tankers that can be on the ocean.

**Write a synonym for <u>regulate</u>.**

_____

**2** Oil sometimes leaks from a tanker. The spilled oil floats on top of the water. Waves wash the oil ashore. The oil covers the **vegetation** on the coast.

**What are some kinds of <u>vegetation</u>?**

_____

_____

_____

**3** Oil companies have the **responsibility** of cleaning up oil spills. They send workers to clean up the mess.

Describe something you take <u>responsibility</u> for in school or at home.

_____

_____

_____

**4** Birds and other animals may be covered with oil after a spill. Some of these animals may be **endangered**. Special soap is used to clean the animals.

What does it mean to say that an animal is <u>endangered</u>?

_____

_____

_____

**5** Workers try to **restore** the ocean and land to their original beauty. They use machines to take oil off the water and the shore. A special material is put on plants to clean them.

Tell about something that you would like to <u>restore</u>.

_____

_____

_____

# Oil Spill in Alaska

## by Richard Stull

My name is Kim. My family and I live in a small town. The town is on the coast of Alaska.

One day after breakfast, my mom and I waved goodbye to my dad. He was heading out to sea on his boat. My dad is a fisherman. As we looked at the ocean, we did not know that something terrible was about to happen.

### Stop Think Write

INFER/PREDICT

**What do you predict this story will tell you about Kim's dad and the Alaska oil spill?**

_____

_____

_____

Mom heard the news on the radio. An oil tanker had drifted too close to shore. Rocks in the shallow water had ripped a hole in the bottom of the tanker. Thousands of gallons of oil were spilling into the ocean.

My dad's boat returned early that afternoon. I ran to the dock to meet him. "The oil has spread for miles," he said. It had covered birds and sea animals. The oil was also being carried ashore by waves. As a result, **vegetation** along the coast was covered with oil.

## Stop | Think | Write

VOCABULARY

What forms of vegetation might be affected by the oil spill?

_____

_____

_____

A group of men and women met at the mayor's office. They wanted to learn more about the oil spill. The mayor told them that government workers were on their way to start cleaning the oil.

Some of the people wanted to help. "It's our duty as citizens to help clean this oil spill," said my mother.

"I agree," said the mayor. "We all live and work here. We should help clean up this mess."

### Stop | Think | Write

Why did the author include details about the town's citizens and mayor?

_____

_____

_____

High school students also wanted to help. They agreed with my mother and the mayor. The students also felt that humans had a **responsibility** to help the wild animals.

"Humans made this mess," one student pointed out. "That is why we owe it to the animals to help them."

Everyone decided that they should help clean up the oil spill.

## Stop | Think | Write

CAUSE AND EFFECT

**Why do the students believe that everyone should help the animals?**

_____

_____

_____

For weeks, everyone worked hard at the cleanup. People cleaned the beaches. They tried to clean as much oil from plants as they could.

They cleaned birds and other animals. Some were soaked with oil. They gave special care to **endangered** animals. These are animals in danger of dying out completely. My dad explained to me that the Eskimo curlew, a bird that lives along the shore, is one such animal.

## Stop  Think  Write

**How might animals become <u>endangered</u>?**

_____

_____

_____

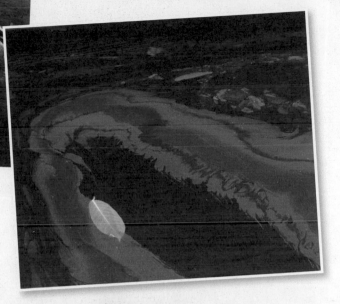

One day, a woman who worked for the government spoke to us. She said that the efforts to **restore** the ocean and shore were ending. "Most of the oil has been removed," she said. She then said that things would be much better in a year or two.

My dad was soon able to fish again. I could play on the beach again. During the cleanup, I hadn't been allowed near the water.

**Stop** **Think** **Write**

INFER/PREDICT

How do you think the people of the town felt after hearing that the cleanup was ending?

_____

_____

_____

The oil spill taught all of us valuable lessons. We learned that human actions can have both bad and good effects. Humans caused the oil spill. People working together cleaned it up.

Maybe the oil companies learned a lesson, too. They should know that they must **regulate** their shipping more carefully. This will help prevent oil spills. Preventing oil spills helps to protect animals and plants on Earth.

## Stop | Think | Write

AUTHOR'S PURPOSE

**What arguments does the author give to persuade the reader about regulating oil shipping?**

_____

_____

_____

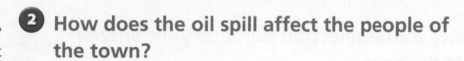

# Look Back and Respond

**1** What effects does the oil spill have on the environment?

_____

_____

_____

**Hint**

For clues, see pages 75, 78, and 79.

**2** How does the oil spill affect the people of the town?

_____

_____

_____

**Hint**

You can find clues on almost every page.

**3** Do you think the people succeeded in cleaning up the oil spill?

_____

_____

_____

**Hint**

For clues, see pages 78 and 79.

**4** What point does the author make about taking responsibility?

_____

_____

_____

**Hint**

You can find clues on pages 76, 77, and 80.

# Be a Reading Detective!

**1** What is the author's purpose in explaining the "circle of life"?

☐ She wants the reader to know more about the Miccosukee.

☐ She wants to encourage people to save the Everglades.

☐ other _____

**Prove It!** What evidence in the selection supports your answer? Check the boxes. ☑ Make notes.

| Evidence | Notes |
|---|---|
| ☐ what the Everglades is like | |
| ☐ dangers the Everglades faces | |
| ☐ | |

## Write About It!

AUTHOR'S PURPOSE

Answer question **1** using evidence from the text.

_____

_____

_____

_____

_____

_____

**2** **Decide whether this statement is a fact or an opinion:**
The Everglades supports many kinds of plants and animals.

☐ a fact      ☐ an opinion

**Prove It!** What evidence in the selection supports your answer?
Check the boxes. ☑  Make notes.

| Evidence | Notes |
|---|---|
| ☐ details about different plants | |
| ☐ details about different animals | |
| ☐ the photos | |

**Write About It!**

FACT AND OPINION

**Answer question** **2** **using evidence from the text.**

_____

_____

_____

_____

_____

_____

_____

# 9

## Search and Rescue Teams

✓ TARGET VOCABULARY

**bundle
clammy
commotion
critical
demolished**

There are many disasters in which search and rescue teams are ❶ _____.
Some teams are made up of local people who know the area well. Some teams are brought in from far away.

Searches take place on mountains. They take place on the ocean. They even take place in the ❷ _____ darkness in caves and mines underground.

82

Weather can cause severe damage. Not only are buildings **3** _____, but people may be trapped in them. Rescue teams search for injured people and take them to safety.

People lost at sea and those caught in snowstorms can be in danger from the cold. Rescue workers **4** _____ these victims in warm blankets.

In a disaster, there will often be a lot of **5** _____. Trees might fall in high winds. People may be shouting. Rescue workers are trained to stay calm in all the confusion.

# The Rescue Helicopter Team
by Laurie Rozakis

## Ready for Rescue

It seemed like a perfect day, so the rescue helicopter team didn't expect to be very busy. The team did almost all of its work in bad weather. That was when people most needed help.

Then the weather started to change. The sky turned dark, and the wind picked up. A storm was blowing in.

A voice came over the radio. The team was told that it was **critical** to get ready. The storm was going to hit hard, and soon.

### Stop | Think | Write

CAUSE AND EFFECT

Why does the helicopter rescue team do most of its work in bad weather?

_____

_____

_____

# Trouble at Sea

Out on the ocean, Manny and Elena had been enjoying a pleasant day of sailing. They hadn't been prepared for the storm that rushed in.

Suddenly clouds covered the sun. The air became **clammy** and cold. The wind howled, and waves pounded the little boat.

Manny tried his best to control the boat, but the storm was too strong. The sails ripped and the mast was **demolished**. Elena rushed into the cabin and sent a distress call over the radio.

**Stop | Think | Write**

VOCABULARY

**What happens to something that is <u>demolished</u>?**

_____

_____

_____

# Rescue at Sea

Elena's call reached the rescue center. The controller found out what the situation was. He quickly alerted the rescue helicopter team and gave them details of the emergency.

The team raced to their helicopter. They started the engines. It was going to be a busy day after all.

**Stop** | **Think** | **Write**

**Why is it going to be a busy day after all?**

_____

_____

_____

The helicopter arrived at the damaged boat in no time. Its crew lowered a basket to the deck. One of the crew went with it. He had to shout his instructions to be heard over all of the **commotion**. He helped Elena into the basket.

The basket was quickly pulled back up. Elena was safe in the helicopter. Then the basket was lowered again to rescue Manny.

## Stop | Think | Write

VOCABULARY

**What causes the <u>commotion</u> at the scene of the rescue?**

_____

_____

_____

The wind continued to howl. The sea continued to crash. The pilot kept the helicopter still, above the little boat. The rescue crew stayed calm.

Manny struggled into the basket and was carried up into the helicopter. It wouldn't be long before a team member would **bundle** him up in a dry blanket. Soon after that, he and Elena would be safe back on land.

**Stop | Think | Write**

**Why do you think a rescue crew needs to stay calm?**

_____

_____

_____

# Another Emergency

The rescue team's work was not over for the day. The controller had another emergency for the team to handle.

The storm had hit hard on land, too. Up in the mountains, a car had skidded out of control. It had crashed into a tree, and the driver was badly hurt. An ambulance would take a while to reach the accident, but there was no time to waste. The rescue helicopter was up in the air again. There was a doctor on board.

**Stop** | **Think** | **Write**

CONCLUSIONS AND GENERALIZATIONS

**Why can't the ambulance rescue the hurt driver?**

# Rescue on Land

Ten minutes later, the helicopter reached the scene. It landed at the side of the highway, and the team ran out to the injured driver. He was quickly lifted onto a stretcher and flown right to the hospital. The pilot landed on the helicopter pad on the hospital roof.

It was all in a day's work for the rescue helicopter team.

## Stop | Think | Write

INFER AND PREDICT

What do you think happens after the helicopter lands on the hospital roof?

_____

_____

_____

# Look Back and Respond

**1** Would working on a rescue helicopter team be dangerous? Explain.

_____

_____

_____

**Hint**

For clues, see pages 87 and 88.

**2** Why are rescue helicopters needed?

_____

_____

_____

**Hint**

There are clues throughout the story.

**3** Why might a hospital have a helicopter pad on the roof, instead of on the ground?

_____

_____

_____

**Hint**

For a clue, think about a hospital that you have seen.

**4** In what ways can bad weather cause disasters?

_____

_____

_____

**Hint**

For clues, see pages 85 and 89.

# Be a Reading Detective!

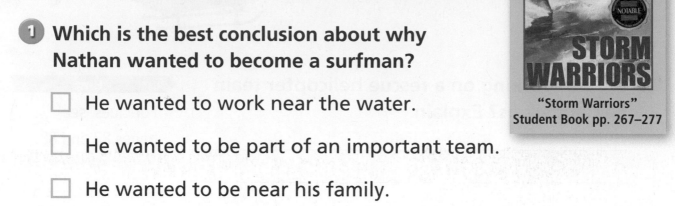

Return to

"Storm Warriors"
Student Book pp. 267–277

**1** Which is the best conclusion about why Nathan wanted to become a surfman?

☐ He wanted to work near the water.

☐ He wanted to be part of an important team.

☐ He wanted to be near his family.

**Prove It!** What evidence in the selection supports your answer? Check the boxes. ✓ Make notes.

| Evidence | Notes |
|---|---|
| ☐ what Nathan thinks and does | |
| ☐ what the surfmen do | |
| ☐ | |

## Write About It!

CONCLUSIONS AND GENERALIZATIONS

Answer question **1** using evidence from the text.

_____

_____

_____

_____

_____

_____

_____

**2** **What does Nathan learn about himself during the rescue?**

☐ He wants to risk his life like the surfmen.

☐ He wants to become a doctor.

☐ other _____

**Prove It!** What evidence in the selection supports your answer?
Check the boxes. ☑️   Make notes.

| Evidence | Notes |
|---|---|
| ☐ what Nathan thinks as he watches the surfmen work | |
| ☐ how he helps the injured sailor | |
| ☐ | |

**Write About It!**

UNDERSTANDING CHARACTERS

**Answer question ② using evidence from the text.**

_____

_____

_____

_____

_____

_____

# Lesson 10

**available**
**detecting**
**ferocious**
**keen**
**unobserved**

# Animals in Danger

**1** Some fish are disappearing. There aren't many left because fishermen catch them. If people do not buy these fish, fishermen might stop catching them. Buying other **available** fish can help fish that are in danger.

**Write the name of a food that is <u>available</u> in your supermarket.**

_____

_____

_____

**2** Scientists watch animals that are endangered. They count the animals to see how many there are. Pandas are often **unobserved**. They are hard to see in the thick forests of China.

**Describe three things that are <u>unobserved</u> by most people in a park.**

_____

_____

_____

**3** You can help wild animals in your area by **detecting** places where they live and go. If you see an animal's home, leave it alone. When you are in the car, look out for animals crossing the road.

**Which senses would you use for <u>detecting</u> your friends while playing hide-and-seek?**

_____

_____

_____

**4** Even **ferocious** animals like great white sharks need help from people to survive. One way to help is by writing letters to lawmakers. Lawmakers can make sure people obey laws that protect sharks. They can try to stop other countries from fishing for sharks.

**Name some other <u>ferocious</u> animals. How can you tell they are ferocious?**

_____

_____

_____

**5** Many young people have a **keen** desire to help animals that are in danger of disappearing. These young people learn about the animals. They teach other people about why the animals need help.

**What is a synonym for <u>keen</u>?**

_____

# Bison Come Back to the Plains

**by Joe Brennan**

## Kings of the Plains

The Great Plains lie in the middle of the United States. They run all the way from the north to the south. These broad, flat lands have few trees. The plains used to be covered with tall grass that would sway in the wind, and people said they looked like oceans of grass.

Until about 150 years ago, bison were the kings of the plains. More than 30 million of these huge animals roamed there. Today, the United States is home to just 80 thousand bison.

### Stop Think Write

MAIN IDEAS AND DETAILS

Why did people say the Great Plains looked like "oceans of grass"?

_____

_____

_____

In the days before European settlers arrived, vast herds of bison grazed on the grass of the plains. After they finished grazing in one area, they would move to another location. Herds moved up to four hundred miles south in the winter, and then back north in the spring. They kept moving in search of **available** fresh grass.

Each year, the bison walked along the same paths. Often they went in a single line. Over time, the bisons' steps wore down the soil. Some paths were worn three feet deep!

## Stop | Think | Write

VOCABULARY

**Why would bison have to travel to find <u>available</u> fresh grass?**

_____

_____

_____

# Hunting Bison

American Indian tribes shared the Great Plains with the bison. Bison were very important to the Plains Indians. They depended on these animals for food, clothing, and shelter.

The bison were not easy to kill. They weighed over 1,000 pounds. They could run as fast as horses. Their hooves and horns were very sharp. Bison used their broad heads to ram their enemies. The Plains Indians had to find ways to kill the dangerous animals without getting hurt themselves.

## Stop | Think | Write

COMPARE AND CONTRAST

What animal does the author compare to bison to show how fast the bison were?

_____

_____

_____

Before the Plains Indians had horses, hunting was difficult. Hunters would sometimes drive a group of bison along a prepared path. The end of the path was a cliff that would be **unobserved** by the bison. They would fall over the edge and die. The Plains Indians could then feed their people. Driving bison, however, was not as easy as it sounds. As people say, you can't drive a bison anywhere it doesn't want to go!

After horses came to America, Plains Indians could hunt on horseback with bows and arrows. They killed only the few bison they needed.

## Stop | Think | Write

CAUSE AND EFFECT

**How did the Plains Indians' hunting methods change after they began using horses?**

_____

_____

_____

## Wasting Nothing

The Plains Indians used every part of the animals they hunted. They dried the meat so that it would last for many weeks without spoiling. Bison skins made warm fur coats and blankets. Plains Indians also stretched the skins over frames made of wooden poles. These tepees provided dry, warm homes and were easy to move from one place to another.

The bones of the bison were used to make tools. Chips of dried bison dung were used as fuel for campfires. The Plains Indians made strong leather from bison skins. They used parts of the animals to make boats and bags.

**Stop** | **Think** | **Write**

MAIN IDEAS AND DETAILS

Write three details that tell how American Indians used different parts of the bison.

_____

_____

_____

# What Happened to the Bison?

When settlers from Europe arrived in the Great Plains, the days of the huge herds were numbered. The settlers killed bison for sport, and they killed them to clear the path for railways. By the 1880s, fewer than one thousand bison were left in all of North America.

Some men and women saved a group of bison that were left. They brought them to a protected area. More bison were raised from that group. Slowly, the number of bison grew.

The government passed laws protecting bison. National parks were created where bison would be cared for and protected. With our help, bison will always have an open place to eat grass and roam free.

## Stop | Think | Write

MAIN IDEAS AND DETAILS

Write two details that describe people's efforts to save bison.

_____

_____

_____

# Bison Facts

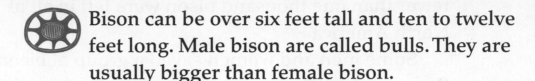 Most bison are dark brown or black. Every once in a while, a white bison is born. Plains Indians thought white bison were very special. They told many stories of the rare white beasts.

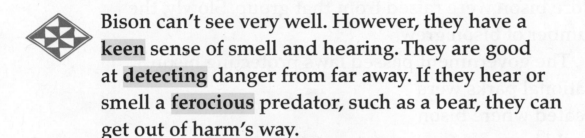 Bison can be over six feet tall and ten to twelve feet long. Male bison are called bulls. They are usually bigger than female bison.

Bison can't see very well. However, they have a **keen** sense of smell and hearing. They are good at **detecting** danger from far away. If they hear or smell a **ferocious** predator, such as a bear, they can get out of harm's way.

## Stop | Think | Write

VOCABULARY

**How would a <u>keen</u> sense of hearing protect an animal?**

_____

_____

_____

# Look Back and Respond

**1** **What is this text mainly about? How can you tell?**

**Hint**

What are most of the section heads about?

_____

_____

_____

**2** **Why were bison paths three feet lower than the ground on either side?**

**Hint**

For a clue, see page 95.

_____

_____

_____

**3** **Why did bison almost disappear from Earth?**

**Hint**

Look for clues on page 99.

_____

_____

_____

**4** **Predict what will happen to bison in the future. Use details from the text to support your answer.**

**Hint**

For a clue, see page 99.

_____

_____

_____

# Be a Reading Detective!

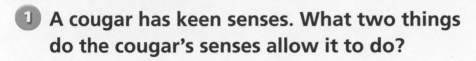

**Return to Cougars**

"Cougars"
Student Book pp. 295–305

**1** A cougar has keen senses. What two things do the cougar's senses allow it to do?

☐ judge the size of a small space

☐ hunt prey during the day or night

☐ teach a kitten how to chew

**Prove It!** What evidence in the selection supports your answer? Check the boxes. ☑ Make notes.

| Evidence | Notes |
|---|---|
| ☐ eyesight | |
| ☐ hearing | |
| ☐ sense of smell | |
| ☐ sense of touch | |

## Write About It!

MAIN IDEAS AND DETAILS

Answer question **1** using evidence from the text.

_____

_____

_____

_____

_____

_____

_____

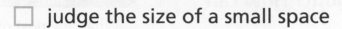

101A

**2** **Which of these events happens last?**

☐ Young cougars lose their spots.

☐ Young cougars are kept hidden by their mother.

☐ Young cougars are able to hunt for themselves.

**Prove It!** What evidence in the selection supports your answer? Check the boxes. ☑ Make notes.

| Evidence | Notes |
|---|---|
| ☐ the text | |
| ☐ photos and captions | |
| ☐ | |

**Write About It!**

SEQUENCE OF EVENTS

Answer question **2** using evidence from the text.

_____

_____

_____

_____

_____

_____

_____

✓ TARGET VOCABULARY

**conduct**
**pressing**
**representatives**
**surveyed**
**viewpoint**

# The Revolutionary War at Sea

**1** During the Revolutionary War, the Patriots and the British had one thing in common. Both had a **pressing** need to control the sea. They had to get supplies to their armies. They had to move soldiers from place to place.

**What might make going to the store pressing?**

_____

_____

_____

**2** Both sides wanted travel to be safe for their ships. The Americans wanted to send **representatives** to other countries. They wanted to ask those countries for help. Getting there was the hard part.

**What do student representatives at your school do?**

_____

_____

**3** Many American sailors joined the fight. They were not part of the official navy. They used their own boats. They decided what they would do. They were in charge of their own **conduct**. They were fighting for their freedom!

**Write a synonym for the word conduct.**

_____

**4** These sailors **surveyed** the seas. They looked for British ships. They captured many British ships and sailors. Losing ships made it hard for the British to keep on fighting.

**If you surveyed the walls of your classroom right now, what would you see?**

_____

_____

**5** The official American Navy did not have many boats. Historians say that is why so many private ones were needed. From their **viewpoint**, the private boats and sailors helped America win the war.

**What viewpoint might the British have had about American sailors?**

_____

_____

_____

# The Story of Bunker's Cove

## by Mia Lewis

Jack Bunker was an old salt. An old salt is a sailor who has sailed on ships for many years. Jack wasn't old, but he had sailed on many ships!

Jack and his sister Comfort lived in Maine. Jack lived on Cranberry Island, near the coast. Comfort and her husband John lived at Norwood's Cove on a farm near the water. Their home was happy and quiet. They felt no **pressing** need to become involved with politics.

### Stop | Think | Write

VOCABULARY

Why did Jack and Comfort feel no <u>pressing</u> need to become involved with politics?

_____

_____

_____

Life in Maine was peaceful. In other parts of New England, though, the colonists were angry with Britain. Colonists had no say in the laws that the British made for them. If they couldn't have **representatives**, colonial Patriots wanted freedom from the British. The British soldiers sailed to America to stop the Patriots. By 1775, the American Revolution had started.

## Stop | Think | Write

CAUSE AND EFFECT

**Why did the British need to send soldiers to the colonies?**

_____

_____

_____

**105**

One day, John and Comfort went to visit friends. While they were gone, a British ship arrived. The British killed the cows on the farm and burned the house. They left a note that said, "Starve!"

Jack was very upset at the **conduct** of the British soldiers. He decided to do something. He and a friend traveled by canoe for many days until they found a big British boat named the *Falmouth Packet*. It was anchored offshore, full of food and supplies. Its crew was on land.

**Stop** **Think** **Write**

VOCABULARY

Why was Jack upset by the <u>conduct</u> of the British soldiers?

_____

_____

_____

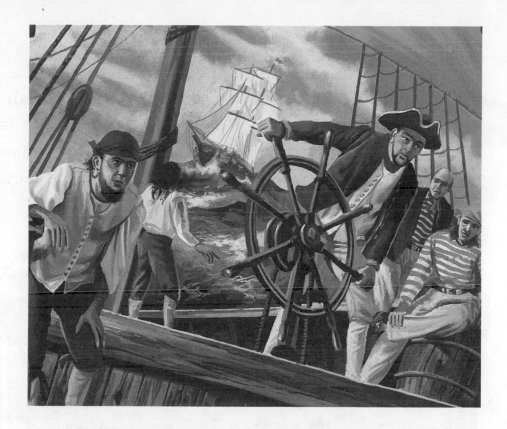

Jack and his friend climbed onto the boat and put up the sails. They sailed to Norwood's Cove and gave his sister all the supplies. Then he decided to hide the boat. He didn't want the British to be able to use it to fight the Patriots.

A crew of friends helped Jack sail the boat out to sea. There were many British warships out there. One captain **surveyed** the sea and saw Jack. He began to chase the slower supply boat. Jack was a fine sailor. He knew how to make the *Falmouth Packet* go fast. Could he go fast enough?

**Stop** **Think** **Write**

CAUSE AND EFFECT

How did Jack manage to take the *Falmouth Packet* so easily?

_____

_____

_____

Jack thought of a special place to hide the boat. He sailed it into a little cove. The British couldn't see where the boat had gone. Then Jack and his friends decided to cut down the masts. The British saw the masts fall. Now they knew where the *Falmouth Packet* was hidden.

**Stop** | **Think** | **Write**

How does Jack's skill as a sailor and knowledge of the coast help him?

_____

_____

_____

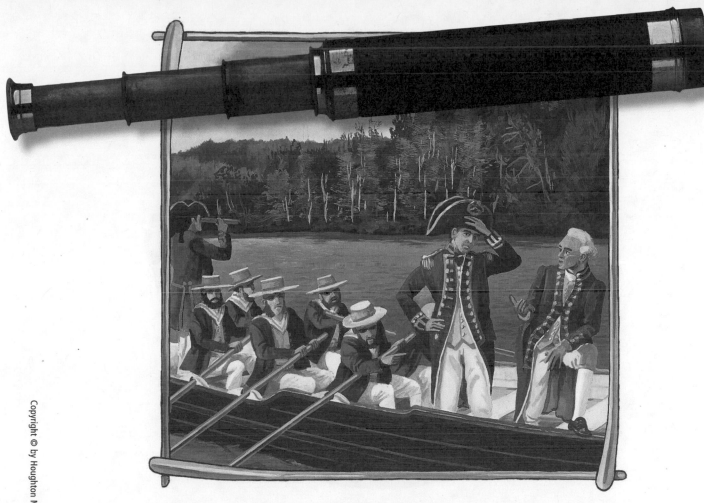

The British captain didn't want to sail into the little cove at first. His **viewpoint** was that the rocks would sink the big ship. Finally, he and some of his men took a small rowboat into the cove. They looked around, but they didn't see Jack or the *Falmouth Packet*.

Jack and his friends had taken the *Falmouth Packet* close to the land. They cut a hole in the bottom of the boat. It sank into the mud. Then they covered it with tree branches and seaweed.

## Stop | Think | Write

INFER AND PREDICT

**Why did Jack and his friends sink the *Falmouth Packet*?**

_____

_____

_____

Jack and his friends escaped in two rowboats. They rowed at night and hid during the day. After a long journey, they finally arrived home.

These daring men helped the Patriots fight the British. The United States eventually won the war. The colonies were free.

Jack didn't stop sailing. He lived to be a really old salt! Today the little cove where Jack hid the *Falmouth Packet* is named Bunker's Cove.

**Stop | Think | Write**

CONCLUSIONS AND GENERALIZATIONS

**What did Jack do after the Revolutionary War was over?**

_____

_____

_____

# Look Back and Respond

**1** What did the British soldiers do that made Jack angry?

_____

_____

_____

**Hint**

For clues, look on page 106.

**2** Why did Jack bring the *Falmouth Packet* to Norwood Cove?

_____

_____

_____

**Hint**

For a clue, see page 107.

**3** Write three words to describe Jack.

_____

_____

_____

**Hint**

You can find clues all through the story.

**4** How did Jack and his friends help the Patriots defeat the British?

_____

_____

_____

**Hint**

Think what would have happened if Jack had NOT taken the British supply ship.

# Be a Reading Detective!

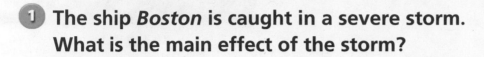 **Return to**

"Dangerous Crossing"
Student Book pp. 327–339

**1** The ship *Boston* is caught in a severe storm. What is the main effect of the storm?

☐ Johnny gets to see a Portuguese man-of-war.

☐ The Adamses never make it to France.

☐ The *Boston* goes hundreds of miles off course.

**Prove It!** What evidence in the selection supports your answer? Check the boxes. ☑ Make notes.

| Evidence | Notes |
|---|---|
| ☐ how long the storm lasts | |
| ☐ the violence of the storm | |
| ☐ how the author describes the end of the storm | |

## Write About It!

CAUSE AND EFFECT

Answer question **1** using evidence from the text.

_____

_____

_____

_____

_____

_____

_____

**2** What is the most important thing the author wants readers to understand about Johnny's father, John Adams?

☐ He gets bored easily.

☐ He cares about justice.

☐ He travels to France.

**Prove It!** What evidence in the selection supports your answer? Check the boxes. ☑ Make notes.

| Evidence | Notes |
|---|---|
| ☐ what Adams says | |
| ☐ the reason for his voyage | |
| ☐ the way the selection ends | |

**Write About It!**

AUTHOR'S PURPOSE

Answer question **2** using evidence from the text.

_____

_____

_____

_____

_____

_____

_____

# Lesson 12

✓ **TARGET VOCABULARY**

advantages
benefit
objected
rebellious
repeal

# 1770s Americans Revolt!

Colonists in America had to pay taxes to the British. There were taxes on such things as glass, paint, paper, and tea. Many colonists **objected** to paying these taxes. They felt that Americans didn't get any **benefit** from the money. It all went to Britain.

**Rebellious** colonists were tired of being told what to do by a government far away. They spoke out against the taxes. They demanded that the British **repeal** the tax laws. Then they would not have to pay taxes to the British.

Britain would not let the colonists govern themselves. Americans wanted change. They started a revolution. When they fought, they had some **advantages** over the British. They knew the land around them. They believed in their cause.

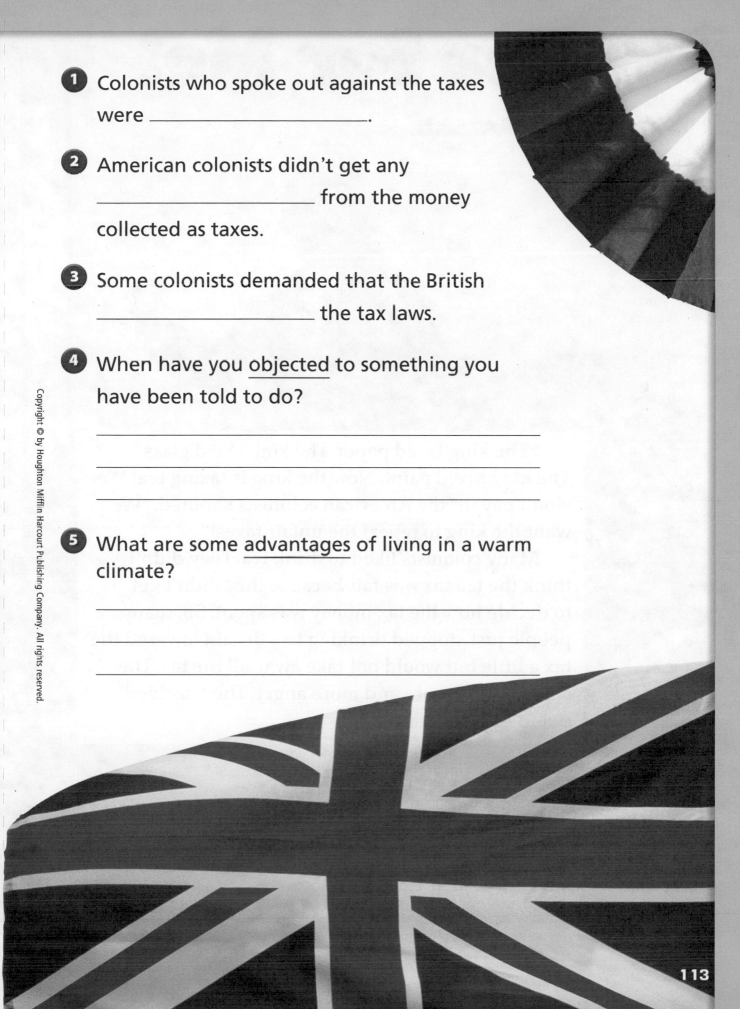

**1** Colonists who spoke out against the taxes were _____.

**2** American colonists didn't get any _____ from the money collected as taxes.

**3** Some colonists demanded that the British _____ the tax laws.

**4** When have you <u>objected</u> to something you have been told to do?

_____

_____

_____

**5** What are some <u>advantages</u> of living in a warm climate?

_____

_____

_____

# No Tea for Me!

## by Laurie Rozakis

"The king taxed paper. The king taxed glass. The king taxed paint. Now the king is taxing tea! We won't pay it!" the American colonists shouted. "We want the king to **repeal** the unfair taxes!"

Many colonists liked to drink tea. They didn't think the tea tax was fair because they didn't get to decide how the tax money was spent. So, many people just stopped drinking tea. Britain lowered the tax a little but would not take away all the tax. The colonists got more and more angry. They decided not to buy any tea at all.

## Stop  Think  Write

CAUSE AND EFFECT

**Why did the colonists think the tea tax was unfair?**

_____

_____

_____

# We Won't Pay!

It was December 16, 1773. More than 7,000 angry colonists stood on the Boston dock. Three big British ships were in the harbor. They carried a lot of tea. The governor told the people to let the ships unload the tea. The colonists **objected** to the order.

The colonists were very angry. If the ships were unloaded, the colonists would have to pay the tea tax. They wanted the ships to leave without unloading. A leader named Samuel Adams held meetings. He told the people not to let the ships unload. The people cheered!

## Stop | Think | Write

VOCABULARY

Why do you think the colonists <u>objected</u> to the governor's order?

_____

_____

_____

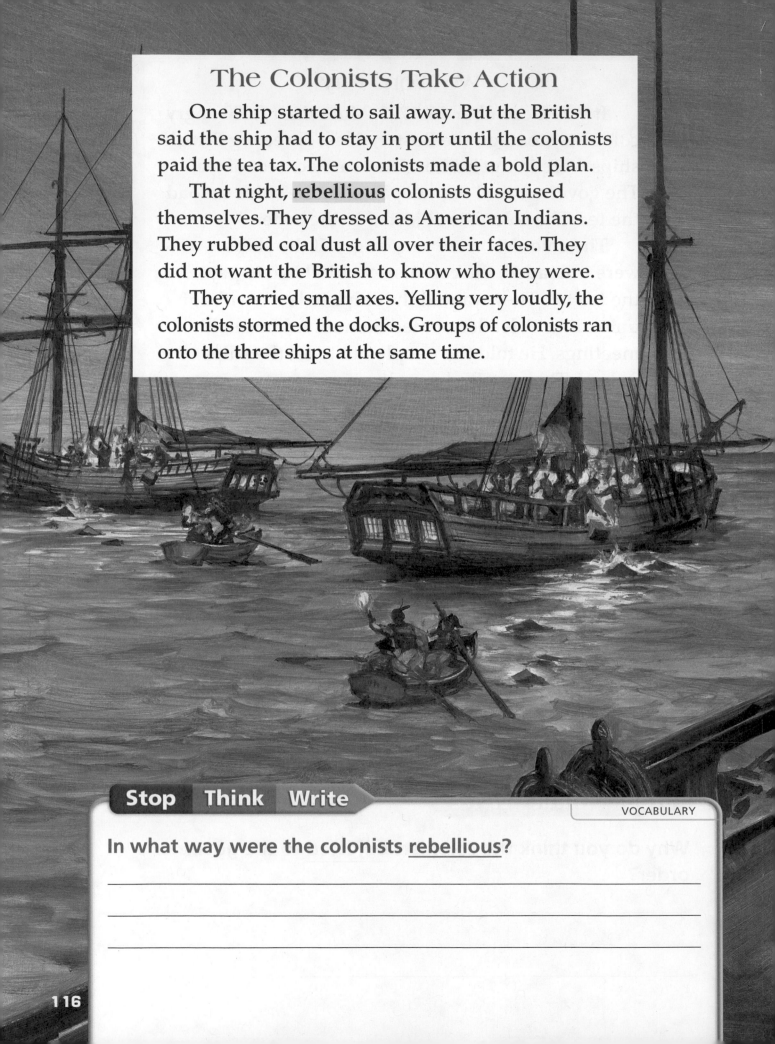

# The Colonists Take Action

One ship started to sail away. But the British said the ship had to stay in port until the colonists paid the tea tax. The colonists made a bold plan.

That night, **rebellious** colonists disguised themselves. They dressed as American Indians. They rubbed coal dust all over their faces. They did not want the British to know who they were.

They carried small axes. Yelling very loudly, the colonists stormed the docks. Groups of colonists ran onto the three ships at the same time.

**Stop** **Think** **Write**

VOCABULARY

In what way were the colonists <u>rebellious</u>?

_____

_____

_____

## A Bold Tea Party

The men got the keys to the storage hatches. They unlocked the doors. They grabbed the chests of tea. They chopped holes in the tea chests. That way, the chests would not float in the water like corks. Their axes crashed into the dry wood. Then they tossed the chests of tea over the sides of the boats.

Some of the tea was still floating in the water the next day. The men beat the crates with paddles to make them sink. They did not want any of the tea to be saved.

**Stop** | **Think** | **Write**

CAUSE AND EFFECT

**Why did the colonists throw all the tea into Boston Harbor?**

_____

_____

_____

## The British Punish the Colonists

British ships in the harbor left the colonists alone. The British king did not. Back in England, King George was very, very angry. He did not like this "tea party" at all. He did not like the way the colonists had acted. Their actions did not have any **benefit** for him or his country.

The king quickly closed Boston Harbor. That meant that no goods at all could reach Boston by ship. King George also took many powers away from the colonists.

**Stop** | **Think** | **Write**

FACT AND OPINION

What was the king's opinion of the colonists' actions? Explain.

_____

_____

_____

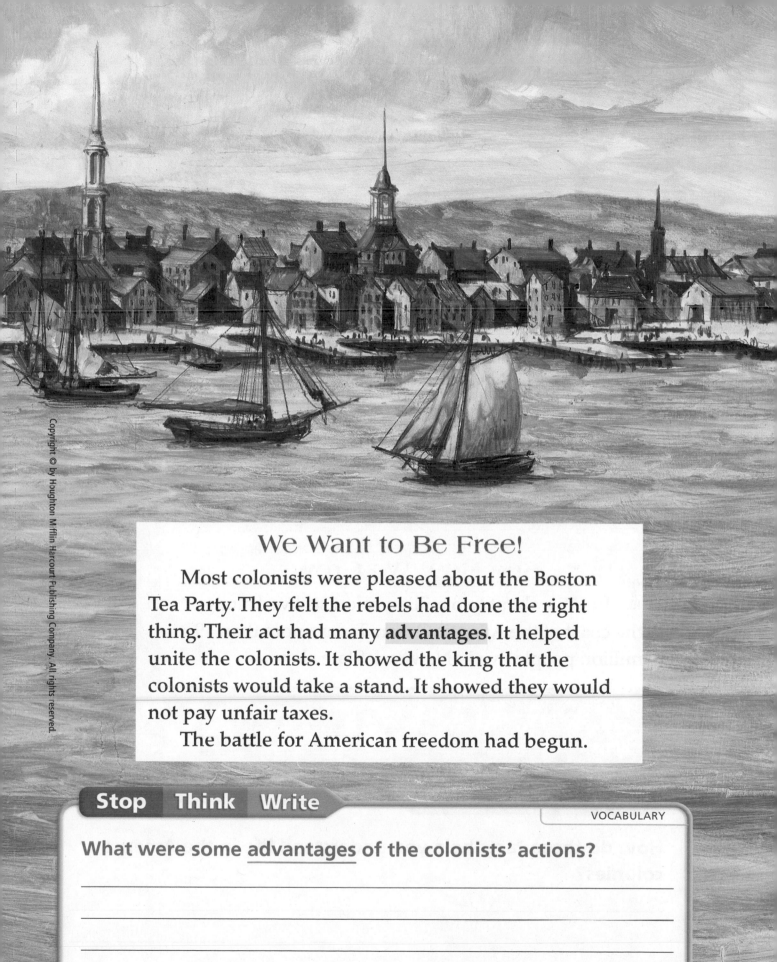

## We Want to Be Free!

Most colonists were pleased about the Boston Tea Party. They felt the rebels had done the right thing. Their act had many **advantages**. It helped unite the colonists. It showed the king that the colonists would take a stand. It showed they would not pay unfair taxes.

The battle for American freedom had begun.

**Stop** **Think** **Write**

VOCABULARY

**What were some advantages of the colonists' actions?**

_____

_____

_____

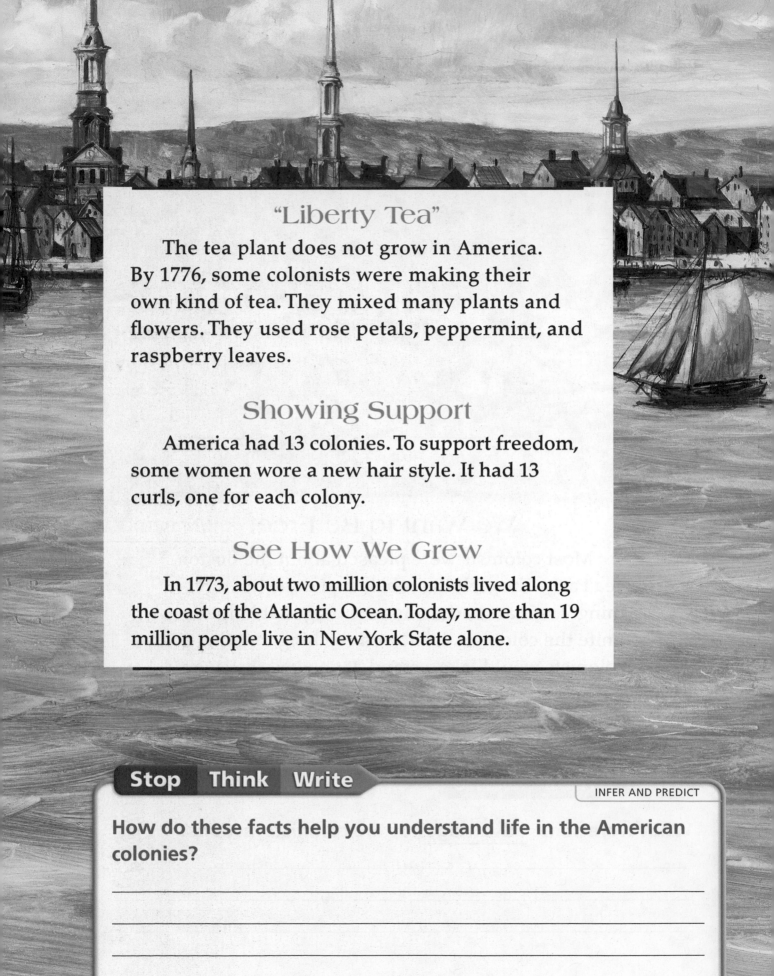

### "Liberty Tea"

The tea plant does not grow in America. By 1776, some colonists were making their own kind of tea. They mixed many plants and flowers. They used rose petals, peppermint, and raspberry leaves.

### Showing Support

America had 13 colonies. To support freedom, some women wore a new hair style. It had 13 curls, one for each colony.

### See How We Grew

In 1773, about two million colonists lived along the coast of the Atlantic Ocean. Today, more than 19 million people live in New York State alone.

**Stop** **Think** **Write**

INFER AND PREDICT

How do these facts help you understand life in the American colonies?

_____

_____

_____

## Look Back and Respond

**1** What was the colonists' opinion of the king's actions?

**Hint**

For a clue, see page 114.

_____

_____

_____

**2** Which facts tell you how the king punished the colonists?

**Hint**

For clues, see page 118.

_____

_____

_____

**3** The Boston Tea Party was the bravest thing the Americans had done. Is this sentence a fact or an opinion? Explain.

**Hint**

Remember: a fact can be proved, but an opinion cannot.

_____

_____

_____

**4** How could the British have supported their opinion that the colonists should pay taxes?

**Hint**

Think about what governments use taxes for.

_____

_____

_____

# Be a Reading Detective!

Return to

"Can't You Make Them Behave, King George?"
Student Book pp. 359–369

**1** Which sentence can you support with details or examples from the selection?

☐ King George was a great king.

☐ King George liked the colonists.

☐ King George tried to control the American colonies.

**Prove It!** What evidence in the selection supports your answer? Check the boxes. ☑ Make notes.

| Evidence | Notes |
|---|---|
| ☐ King George's thoughts | |
| ☐ King George's actions in taxing | |
| ☐ King George's military actions | |

## Write About It!

FACT AND OPINION

Answer question **1** using evidence from the text.

_____

_____

_____

_____

_____

_____

**2** **What is one main idea of this selection?**

☐ A strong king can force his people to obey him.

☐ If people do not believe their government is fair, they will rebel.

☐ Americans have never liked tea very much.

**Prove It!** What evidence in the selection supports your answer? Check the boxes. ☑ Make notes.

| Evidence | Notes |
|---|---|
| ☐ what King George said and thought | |
| ☐ how Americans responded to the king's actions | |
| ☐ the result of the American Revolution | |

**Write About It!**

MAIN IDEAS AND DETAILS

**Answer question** **2** **using evidence from the text.**

_____

_____

_____

_____

_____

_____

_____

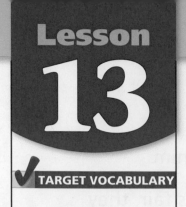

foes
formal
retreat
revolution
strategy

# Women in Revolutionary Times

**1** War isn't difficult just for soldiers. The **revolution** in the colonies was hard on families. The women had to do all the men's work while they were away.

**What is the difference between a <u>revolution</u> and a small change?**

_____

_____

_____

**2** Some Americans supported the Patriots in the war. They wanted the colonies to be free. Their **foes** were the British. Other Americans were Loyalists. They backed the British. They were loyal to King George.

**Write a synonym for the word <u>foes</u>.**

_____

**3** The war was long and hard. It took time to move troops from place to place. The generals had to make plans. They had to have a good **strategy** for every battle.

What kinds of details do you think would go into a general's <u>strategy</u> for a battle?

_____

_____

_____

**4** Sometimes the British army marched toward a city. The people in the city had to decide. Should they stay? Should they go? Many would **retreat** to safety before the army arrived.

Would you <u>retreat</u> if the British army were coming to your city? Explain your answer.

_____

_____

_____

**5** Many men joined the army. There was often no time for **formal** training. The men had to start fighting right away. On top of this, the army was short of supplies. Some soldiers didn't even have shoes.

In general, do you think it is useful for soldiers to receive <u>formal</u> training? Why or why not?

_____

_____

_____

# Women
### of the American Revolution

by Mia Lewis

Men did most of the fighting against the British. Women, young and old, played a part, too. They did many things to help win the war.

Women stopped buying British goods. They made their own cloth. They kept their family farms running when the men were off fighting.

Women gave food and shelter to the troops. They gave the men advice and support. Some women worked as spies. A few even took up arms.

## Stop    Think    Write

CONCLUSIONS AND GENERALIZATIONS

In general, did women help the Patriots as supporters or as fighters? Explain.

_____

_____

_____

**Lydia Darragh** lived in Philadelphia. The British took control of the city in 1777. Many Patriots fled, but Lydia and her family stayed behind.

General Howe led the British troops. He and his men set up a meeting using the Darraghs' dining room. Lydia and her family were told to go to sleep. Lydia stayed awake, however. She listened at the keyhole and heard the British talk. They were planning a surprise attack on the Patriots!

## Stop Think Write

CONCLUSIONS AND GENERALIZATIONS

**What conclusions about Lydia can you draw from her actions?**

_____

_____

_____

Lydia said she needed flour. The British gave her a pass to leave the city. She dropped off her flour sack at the mill and kept walking. She walked until she met her friend Thomas Craig.

Craig was in the colonial army. Lydia told him what she had heard. Then she picked up her flour and went home. Craig passed on the warning.

The Americans were ready for their **foes** when the British arrived. Howe had to **retreat** without firing a shot. Lydia had saved the day.

## Stop | Think | Write

VOCABULARY

**Why were the Americans ready when their <u>foes</u> attacked?**

_____

_____

_____

**Deborah Sampson** wanted to fight the British. Women could not join the army, so her **strategy** was to go to war as a man! She signed up as "Robert Shurtleff." She dressed as a man, and she fought as a man. No one in the army knew her secret.

Deborah was in several battles. She was wounded more than once. She let the army doctor treat a deep cut on her head. She hid her other wounds, afraid that doctors would find out she was a woman.

**Stop** **Think** **Write**

VOCABULARY

**Describe Deborah Sampson's strategy for fighting the British.**

_____

_____

_____

127

One day Deborah got really sick. She had a high fever. A doctor treated her and found out her secret. He kept quiet about it. He treated her until she was well again.

"Robert Shurtleff" got an honorable discharge from the army. Deborah put her own clothes back on and went home. She later married and had three children. Deborah asked for a pension for her service. She was the first woman to get an army pension.

**Stop** **Think** **Write**

CONCLUSIONS AND GENERALIZATIONS

**What would you say about women who fought disguised as men?**

_____

_____

_____

Abigail Adams was the wife of John Adams. John was an important Founding Father. He went to France to speak for America. He was our first vice president and our second president.

John Adams was a hero. He helped bring about a **revolution** in America. Abigail was a hero, too! She stood up for the rights of women. She gave her husband advice. He always listened to her, and he said that Abigail was one of his best advisers.

## Stop | Think | Write

UNDERSTANDING CHARACTERS

How can you tell that Abigail Adams was a good partner for her husband, John Adams?

_____

_____

_____

Sometimes John Adams was away from home. So Abigail and John wrote letters. They were friendly letters and weren't too **formal**. They included news and advice. Abigail and John wrote many letters to each other over the years.

One letter from Abigail to John is famous. John was away for a long time, working with the men in Congress. He was planning for the future of the United States. Abigail sent him a letter. It said, "Remember the ladies!"

## Stop | Think | Write

**What do you think Abigail Adams meant when she said, "Remember the ladies!"?**

_____

_____

_____

# Look Back and Respond

**1** **What was so important about what Lydia Darragh did?**

**Hint**

For clues, see pages 125 and 126.

_____

_____

_____

**2** **Was Deborah Sampson a brave soldier?**

**Hint**

For clues, see page 127.

_____

_____

_____

**3** **How did Abigail Adams help her country?**

**Hint**

For clues, see pages 129 and 130.

_____

_____

_____

**4** **In general, how would you describe Patriot women?**

**Hint**

Look for clues on every page.

_____

_____

_____

# Be a Reading Detective!

Return to

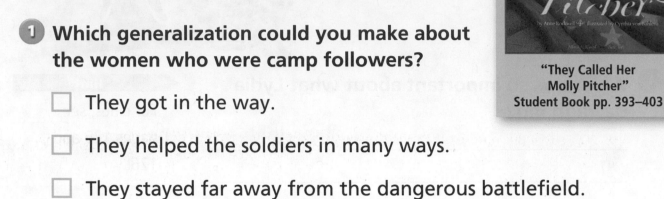

**"They Called Her Molly Pitcher"**
Student Book pp. 393–403

**1** **Which generalization could you make about the women who were camp followers?**

☐ They got in the way.

☐ They helped the soldiers in many ways.

☐ They stayed far away from the dangerous battlefield.

**Prove It!** What evidence in the selection supports your answer? Check the boxes. ☑ Make notes.

| Evidence | Notes |
|---|---|
| ☐ details about what camp followers did | |
| ☐ Molly's actions | |
| ☐ | |

IN CONGRESS. JULY 4, 1776

The unanimous Declaration of the thirteen united States of America

**Write About It!**

CONCLUSIONS AND GENERALIZATIONS

Answer question **1** using evidence from the text.

_____
_____
_____
_____
_____
_____
_____

**2** **Why did the British army retreat from the battleground?**

☐ They hadn't expected the Americans to fight so well.

☐ They refused to fight against women.

☐ George Washington's soldiers had better weapons.

**Prove It!** What evidence in the selection supports your answer? Check the boxes. ☑ Make notes.

| Evidence | Notes |
|---|---|
| ☐ details about the two armies | |
| ☐ details about George Washington | |
| ☐ details about the retreat | |

**Write About It!**

CAUSE AND EFFECT

Answer question **2** using evidence from the text.

_____

_____

_____

_____

_____

_____

_____

apprentice
aspects
contributions
influential
provisions

# Life at Valley Forge

**Check the answer.**

**1** The most _____ man at Valley Forge was George Washington, the general of the Continental Army.

☐ **pressing**   ☐ **influential**   ☐ **shaken**

**2** A young man learning to shoe horses in camp would be an _____ to a blacksmith.

☐ **commotion**   ☐ **apprentice**   ☐ **bundle**

**3** Building huts, training for battle, and marching were all _____ of a soldier's life at Valley Forge.

☐ **aspects**   ☐ **provisions**   ☐ **representatives**

**4** At Valley Forge, there were not nearly enough _____, such as food and clothing.

☐ **aspects**   ☐ **advantages**   ☐ **provisions**

**5** One of the greatest _____ to the army was made by Baron von Steuben, who taught the soldiers to fight as a single force.

☐ **representatives** ☐ **contributions** ☐ **provisions**

**6** What are some of the <u>aspects</u> of your life as a student?

_____

_____

_____

**7** Describe how someone was <u>influential</u> in changing the way you think.

_____

_____

_____

**8** What <u>contributions</u> do you make to your community?

_____

_____

_____

# Nero Hawley's Dream

by Joe Brennan

The American Revolution had started. All over the country, Patriots were fighting for freedom. The British were fighting back.

At first, not everyone was allowed to join the Patriot cause. Many Patriot leaders didn't want to allow free or enslaved blacks to take part. Then the British offered freedom to any enslaved man who would join their side.

**Stop** **Think** **Write**

INFER AND PREDICT

Why might Patriot leaders not want everyone to join the army?

_____

_____

_____

This worried the Patriots. They needed more men. So they allowed free blacks to join up. Some white men who didn't want to go to war sent slaves in their place as well.

Nero Hawley was one of those enslaved men. He had worked in a sawmill in Connecticut. In the fall of 1777, his master sent him to join the army.

**Stop | Think | Write**

CAUSE AND EFFECT

**How did enslaved men end up fighting with the Patriots?**

_____

_____

_____

**135**

The Patriots promised to free any slaves who fought on their side. Throughout the war, Hawley held on to this promise of freedom. He looked forward to the day he would no longer be enslaved.

Some **aspects** of army life were new to Hawley. As a soldier, he was paid a small amount each month. Before, he hadn't been paid. He ate and worked with other soldiers, black and white. Before, he had only worked with other enslaved people.

**Stop** **Think** **Write**

VOCABULARY

What <u>aspects</u> of army life were new to Hawley?

_____

_____

_____

_____

136

Hawley was sent to Pennsylvania. There he joined General George Washington's troops. Washington was one of the most **influential** leaders in the war. He commanded a huge army of soldiers.

Washington ordered his troops to set up camp at Valley Forge. As the army made camp, snow began to fall. It kept falling. The soldiers knew that the coming winter would be long and hard.

## Stop | Think | Write

VOCABULARY

**What made Washington an <u>influential</u> leader in the war?**

_____

_____

_____

_____

**137**

The winter at Valley Forge was even harder than the soldiers had expected. Hawley shared a hut with twelve other soldiers. The snow fell and then melted. Then more snow fell. It melted. The men couldn't keep dry. The army had begun to run out of **provisions**. There was hardly any food or clothing. Many soldiers had no shoes, and the huts were freezing.

**Stop** | **Think** | **Write**

CAUSE AND EFFECT

Why couldn't the soldiers keep dry?

_____

_____

_____

_____

There were about 500 camp followers at Valley Forge. They were wives, sisters, and children of the men. They made important **contributions** to the army. They took care of wounded soldiers. They cooked and did laundry. They fetched water.

Even so, nearly 3,000 soldiers died of sickness. Nero Hawley was one of the lucky survivors.

## Stop | Think | Write

INFER AND PREDICT

**How else might the camp followers have helped the soldiers?**

_____

_____

_____

_____

In October 1781, the long, terrible war finally ended. The British surrendered. The colonies were free to rule themselves.

Nero Hawley's dream of freedom came true. He had survived many battles and returned to Connecticut a free man. He trained as an **apprentice** and became a skilled brick maker. Hawley lived to be 75 years old.

**Stop** **Think** **Write**

SEQUENCE OF EVENTS

**Did Hawley spend the winter at Valley Forge before or after October 1781? Explain.**

_____

_____

_____

# Look Back and Respond

**1** Who was in charge of the army that Nero Hawley joined?

**Hint**

For a clue, see page 137.

_____

_____

_____

**2** What happened to Nero Hawley after he came home from the war?

**Hint**

For a clue, see page 140.

_____

_____

_____

**3** What caused so many deaths at Valley Forge?

**Hint**

For clues, see pages 138 and 139.

_____

_____

_____

**4** Write these events of Hawley's life in order: he works as a brick maker; he camps at Valley Forge; he works in a sawmill; he joins Washington's army.

**Hint**

For clues, thumb through the story.

_____

_____

_____

# Be a Reading Detective!

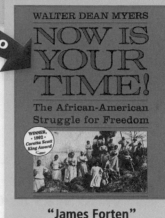

Return to

**WALTER DEAN MYERS**
**NOW IS YOUR TIME!**
The African-American Struggle for Freedom

WINNER · 1992 · Coretta Scott King Award

"James Forten"
Student Book pp. 421–431

**1** **Which event took place before the sea battle with the _Active_?**

☐ The _Royal Louis_ surrendered.

☐ Forten did odd jobs for Robert Bridges.

☐ Forten was imprisoned on the _Jersey_.

**Prove It!** What evidence in the selection supports your answer?
Check the boxes. ☑   Make notes.

| Evidence | Notes |
|---|---|
| ☐ the illustrations | |
| ☐ details from before the sea battle | |
| ☐ details from after the sea battle | |

**Write About It!**

SEQUENCE OF EVENTS

Answer question **1** using evidence from the text.

_____

_____

_____

_____

_____

_____

_____

**2** **Which of the following is an opinion?**

☐ James Forten was not a hero.

☐ Forten learned to read at a Quaker school.

☐ Forten became a wealthy man.

**Prove It!** What evidence in the selection supports your answer?
Check the boxes. ☑ Make notes.

| Evidence | Notes |
|---|---|
| ☐ the author's idea of a hero | |
| ☐ details about Forten's education | |
| ☐ details about Forten's later life | |

**Write About It!**

FACT AND OPINION

**Answer question 2 using evidence from the text.**

_____

_____

_____

_____

_____

_____

_____

✓ **TARGET VOCABULARY**

**efficient**
**organize**
**personally**
**rural**
**tedious**

# Children *of the* 1700s

In the 1700s, children dressed like their parents. They didn't get new shoes often, as shoes were expensive. All shoes were the same whether they were for the left or the right foot. It was easy to **organize** them!

Many towns didn't have a school. If they did, children from ages six through twelve would share the same room. It wasn't a very **efficient** way to learn!

Most children had to work doing dull chores, and they found the work **tedious**. Boys started to learn a trade at the age of nine. Girls would make cloth, candles, and soap at home.

Many colonists lived on **rural** farms. Even very young children in these areas worked hard in the fields.

Boys as young as twelve served as drummers in the army during the Revolution. The drummer would **personally** lead the soldiers into battle.

**1** Having children of all ages share a schoolroom is not a very _____ way to learn.

**2** It is easy to _____ your shoes if they all look exactly the same.

**3** Much of the work that children had to do was _____.

**4** What is something that most people like, but which you <u>personally</u> do not like?

_____

_____

_____

**5** What can you expect to see in a <u>rural</u> area?

_____

_____

_____

# The Carpenter and the Drummer Boy

**by Duncan Searl**

John Potter gathered planks for his uncle's new ship. He was only twelve, but he was already a good carpenter. He had **personally** helped build three ships at his uncle's boatyard in Bristol Harbor, Rhode Island.

Those ships had all been burned. John's uncle was a Patriot, and the British were at war with Patriots. Earlier that year, redcoats had marched into Bristol and set the ships on fire.

John and his uncle were not discouraged. They were building a new ship. When it was finished, they would sail again. Maybe they would fight the redcoats in it!

## Stop Think Write

CAUSE AND EFFECT

**Why would the British burn the Patriots' ships?**

_____

_____

_____

Thomas Strand was British. He was a drummer boy with his father's regiment at Newport, Rhode Island. Wherever the soldiers marched, Thomas led the way. A long line of redcoats followed his drum's sharp rat-a-tat-tat-tat.

"Thomas," the British major called one morning. "Assemble the men!" Thomas began a long drumroll. The redcoats rushed to **organize** themselves into position.

"We're heading to Bristol!" the major said.

## Stop  Think  Write

VOCABULARY

How might soldiers <u>organize</u> themselves into position?

_____

_____

_____

The march to Bristol was long, hot, and dusty. Thomas did not feel well. Usually, he loved nothing more than drumming a steady marching beat. Today this chore seemed **tedious**.

In Bristol, John Potter was alone in the boatyard. He saw the British soldiers coming, and tried to run, but it was too late. The redcoats quickly captured him and tied his hands.

The soldiers were **efficient**. It took them no time to set fire to the new ship. Then they started the march back to Newport, with John as their prisoner.

**Stop  Think  Write**

VOCABULARY

In what way are the soldiers <u>efficient</u>?

_____

_____

_____

The smoke from the burning ship had brought tears to John's eyes. He wouldn't be sailing with his uncle anytime soon. Worse yet, he was a prisoner. What would the British do with him? John started to feel better when he realized that the march would take them right past his home. Maybe he would catch a glimpse of his mother or sister before going to a British prison.

Thomas Strand was feeling worse and worse. As he led the redcoats along the rural road, he became hungry and tired. Gradually his drumming slowed. Then it stopped completely.

**Stop** **Think** **Write**

COMPARE AND CONTRAST

**What are the different reasons that the two boys feel bad?**

_____

_____

_____

As the redcoats approached John's farmhouse, Thomas fainted and fell to the ground. The major sent two of his men to the house to ask for water.

At first, Mrs. Potter and her daughter Eliza were not anxious to help the redcoats. Then they saw the sick drummer boy lying in the road. "He's no older than our John," Eliza said to her mother. They brought some bread and tea out to Thomas.

Stop | Think | Write

CAUSE AND EFFECT

**Why do Mrs. Potter's and Eliza's feelings about helping the redcoats change?**

_____

_____

_____

Of course, it wasn't long before Mrs. Potter spotted her son. "John!" she called, rushing toward him. "Why are you here with the redcoats?"

"I'm their prisoner, Mother," he replied softly.

Mrs. Potter turned angrily to the major. "What do you mean by this, sir? What right do you have to make my son your prisoner?"

"It is the king's order, Madam," the major answered. "Burn the ships at Bristol and take the Patriots prisoner. That is what we were ordered to do."

## Stop | Think | Write

INFER AND PREDICT

**Why is Mrs. Potter surprised that John is a prisoner?**

_____

_____

_____

John's sister Eliza spoke in a soft voice. "I know the king would be grateful that we helped his drummer. I think he would show his thanks by freeing my brother now."

"I'm not sure about the king," said the major, "but I will release your brother."

John was untied and freed. He and his mother promised to return Thomas to Newport when he felt better.

Later that day, John and Eliza rowed Thomas back to Newport. "When the war is over," said Thomas, "I will come back here. Maybe I can help you build a new ship."

"Maybe you can," said John.

## Stop | Think | Write

Do you think John and Thomas could be friends after the war? Explain.

_____

_____

_____

# Look Back and Respond

**1** **Why is Thomas Strand a drummer boy for the British?**

Hint

For a clue, see page 145.

_____

_____

_____

**2** **Compare how Mrs. Potter and Eliza act when they find that John is a prisoner.**

Hint

For clues, see pages 149 and 150.

_____

_____

_____

**3** **What does John Potter expect to happen to him, and what actually happens to him?**

Hint

For clues, see pages 147 and 150.

_____

_____

_____

**4** **Why do you think the major decides to free John in the end?**

Hint

For clues, see pages 149 and 150.

_____

_____

_____

# Be a Reading Detective!

**Return to**

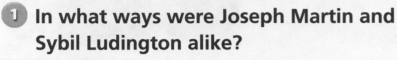

**WE WERE THERE, TOO!**
YOUNG PEOPLE IN U.S. HISTORY
PHILLIP HOOSE

"We Were There, Too!"
Student Book pp. 449–461

**1** **In what ways were Joseph Martin and Sybil Ludington alike?**

☐ They were both from New England.

☐ The both fought for years.

☐ They were both teenagers when they took action.

☐ other _____

**Prove It!** What evidence in the selection supports your answer?
Check the boxes. ☑  Make notes.

| Evidence | Notes |
|---|---|
| ☐ details about Martin | |
| ☐ details about Ludington | |
| ☐ | |

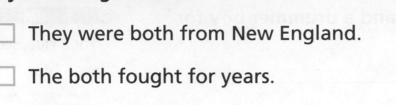

**Write About It!**

COMPARE AND CONTRAST

Answer question **1** using evidence from the text.

_____

_____

_____

_____

_____

_____

_____

**2** **Which generalization is supported by the selection?**

☐ Young people did not take part in the American Revolution.

☐ People who write about their actions are honored more than those who don't.

☐ The fight for freedom takes place on and off the battlefield.

**Prove It!** What evidence in the selection supports your answer? Check the boxes. ☑ Make notes.

| Evidence | Notes |
|---|---|
| ☐ what Ludington and Martin did | |
| ☐ the dangers they faced | |
| ☐ | |

## Write About It!

CONCLUSIONS AND GENERALIZATIONS

**Answer question 2 using evidence from the text.**

_____

_____

_____

_____

_____

_____

_____

**episodes
incredibly
launch
mental
thumbed**

# Making Movies

**1** A film director decides to make a show. He will **launch** the new project as soon as possible. He hopes to get started by June. He can start as soon as he has chosen his lead actors.

**What would you need to do to launch a video club at your school?**

_____

_____

_____

**2** A director flips through the pages. He reads the first scenes. After he has **thumbed** through the script, he reads it in detail.

**If you thumbed through a magazine, how long would it take you? Would it take a long time or a short time?**

_____

_____

_____

**3** The director makes a **mental** picture of the setting. He can see the whole thing in his head. He pictures the scenes and thinks through all the details.

If you have a <u>mental</u> picture of something, how can you share it with someone else?

_____

_____

_____

**4** The show will have lots of action. It will be **incredibly** exciting. The audience will hardly believe their eyes.

Write another word that means the same as <u>incredibly</u>.

_____

**5** There will be five **episodes**. Each episode will tell a story, but all the stories will be connected. The same characters will appear in each episode.

If you made a TV series of your life so far, how many <u>episodes</u> would it have? What would each episode be about?

_____

_____

_____

# Making a Movie
by Mia Lewis

All the members of the video club were in the film studio of Westlake School. It was their first meeting since the club decided to launch a new project.

"We are going to make our own movie," said Sally.

"We'll base it on a story we write ourselves," said Jin.

"We'll have actors," said Wanda.

"We'll have sets," said Julio.

"We'll have everything," said Talia.

"It is going to be incredibly great!" said Sally.

## Stop | Think | Write

AUTHOR'S PURPOSE

Why do you think the author shows every person in the club speaking? You can give more than one reason.

_____

_____

_____

The members of the club were very excited.

"I think our movie should have **episodes**," said Talia. "It can be like a TV series."

"That's a good idea," said Wanda. "But let's figure out the first episode before we think about any others. The first thing we need is a story!"

"I have a story here," said Jin. He took out a notebook and opened it up. "I wrote it this weekend when I was supposed to be raking the lawn. It is very exciting! I even drew a few pictures."

**Stop** **Think** **Write**

VOCABULARY

In what ways are <u>episodes</u> in a TV series connected?

_____

_____

_____

155

Julio **thumbed** through the pages of Jin's story. He read it quickly. He looked at the drawings. He liked the story! Already he had a clear **mental** picture of what the movie would look like.

Julio passed the notebook to Sally, and she started to read.

"This is fantastic!" said Julio. "It will make a great movie!"

"What's it about?" asked Talia.

"It's a story about a group of kids who go hiking," answered Julio. "They are walking along, very close to a river."

"Then Pablo falls in!" said Sally, looking up from the notebook. "He is messing around by the water's edge. He is running too fast. He trips and falls."

## Stop | Think | Write

**What do you think of when you make a <u>mental</u> picture of a river?**

_____

_____

_____

"Yes! He falls right into some deep water. The river is very fast. It washes him downstream," said Julio.

"His friends are all scared," said Sally. "They can't see him anymore."

"They rush along the shore looking for him," said Julio. "The river has taken him. He washes up against a rock far downstream."

## Stop | Think | Write

**Why does the author have Sally and Julio tell the story instead of Jin?**

_____

_____

_____

"That's not all!" added Jin. "When Pablo tries to swim out of the river, he sees a bear sitting on the bank."

"He's stuck," said Julio. "He can't stay in the water forever. He's too cold. He can't go out near the bear."

"He dips his head underwater and holds his breath. He hides behind the rock. After a while, the bear goes away," said Jin.

"His friends arrive," said Julio. "They pull him out."

Talia's eyes were wide. Her mouth was hanging open. Wanda was quiet.

**Stop** **Think** **Write**

AUTHOR'S PURPOSE

**Why do you think the author tells about Talia's eyes and mouth?**

_____

_____

_____

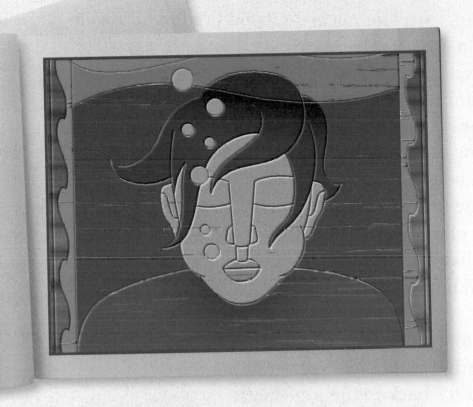

"Wow!" said Talia. "That's quite a story. It sure would make a great movie."

"I can picture the scene with the bear!" said Sally. "We could have scary music in the background. The bear can growl and splash in the water."

"Pablo should look pale and exhausted when he finally gets pulled from the water," said Julio.

"Yes," said Jin. "That's perfect. Guess what? I already have some ideas for other episodes."

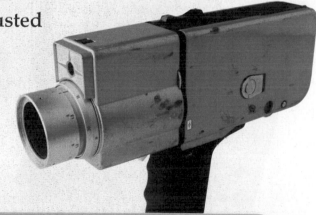

**Stop** **Think** **Write**

ANALYZE/EVALUATE

**What do you think of the video club's plans? What are they forgetting?**

_____

_____

_____

**159**

"Jin, your story is great," said Wanda. "It would make a great movie. However, there are a few problems. First of all, we live in the city! The only wild animals here are pigeons and some stray cats. The only body of water is the public swimming pool. So how are we going to make a movie with a river and a bear?"

The others looked at each other blankly and scratched their heads.

Wanda continued. "Jin, save your story for Hollywood. For our video club, I'm afraid it's back to the drawing board!"

**Stop** **Think** **Write**

CONCLUSIONS AND GENERALIZATIONS

**What does Wanda mean when she says the video club has to go "back to the drawing board"?**

_____

_____

_____

## Look Back and Respond

**1** How would you describe Julio and Sally?

_____

_____

_____

**Hint**

For clues, see pages 156 and 157.

**2** How does the author show that this video club is not very experienced in planning or making movies?

_____

_____

_____

**Hint**

Look for clues on pages 155 to 159.

**3** What clue does the author give early in the story that Wanda is the most practical of all the club members?

_____

_____

_____

**Hint**

See page 155.

**4** What does Wanda mean when she tells Jin to save his story for Hollywood?

_____

_____

_____

**Hint**

Think about what happens in Hollywood.

# Be a Reading Detective!

Return to

"Lunch Money"
Student Book pp. 483–493

**1** Why do you think the author showed the process for making a 16-page comic book?

☐ to keep readers from trying it themselves

☐ to show how important making comics is to Greg

☐ other _____

**Prove It!** What evidence in the story supports your answer? Check the boxes. ☑ Make notes.

| Evidence | Notes |
|---|---|
| ☐ how Greg learns about the process | |
| ☐ illustrations and labels | |

**Write About It!**

AUTHOR'S PURPOSE

Answer question **1** using evidence from the text.

_____

_____

_____

_____

_____

_____

_____

**2** **Which sentence best describes Greg?**

☐ He wants to become a famous artist.

☐ He cares for money more than he cares about his art.

☐ He is a hardworking artist who wants to earn money.

**Prove It!** What evidence in the story supports your answer? Check the boxes. ☑ Make notes.

| Evidence | Notes |
|---|---|
| ☐ details about how carefully Greg works | |
| ☐ details about Greg's sales goal | |
| ☐ details about how many comics Greg sells | |

**Write About It!**

CONCLUSIONS AND GENERALIZATIONS

Answer question **2** using evidence from the text.

_____

_____

_____

_____

_____

_____

_____

**161B**

# How to Write a Science Fiction Story

Science-fiction authors have always **1** _____ that what they describe might never take place. So, write a story about events that might or might not happen in our world.

Many science-fiction stories have **2** _____ readers with original ideas. Follow that lead. Place characters in new situations. The sky's the limit for a plot!

Include some **③** _____
in your story. Not knowing what will happen
next will keep your readers glued to the page.

One major part of a science-fiction story
is a **④** _____ that isn't
possible in real life. In your story, a character
might travel through time or to a city on the
bottom of the ocean.

People have **⑤** _____
many kinds of science-fiction stories. Some
have been made into science-fiction television
shows. Perhaps your story will be made into
a movie!

# In the Year 2525

## by Richard Stull

Vacations in the year 2525 are not what they used to be. In the past, people packed a car and drove for hours or days. Now people can travel millions of miles without taking a step. They can also travel far back in time.

The Ortiz family wanted to take such a vacation. The first step was a visit to the office of Virtual Vacations. There, they talked with a travel agent named Jill.

**Stop** **Think** **Write**

STORY STRUCTURE

As the story begins, what is the Ortiz family doing?

_____

_____

_____

"We want to have lots of fun," said Mr. Ortiz.

"We also want to see strange sights," said Mrs. Ortiz.

"I have the perfect **destination** for you," said Jill. "You're going to Volcano Vacationland!"

Jill explained that Volcano Vacationland was in the distant past. She said that it had pools heated by hot lava and lots of rides for the kids. "You'll also see active volcanoes and dinosaurs," she said. "Of course, the trip is completely safe."

## Stop | Think | Write

VOCABULARY

**Why does Jill think that Volcano Vacationland would be a good <u>destination</u> for the Ortiz family?**

_____

_____

_____

Jill led the Ortizes into the Virtual Vacation Room. In this room, the setting and feel of a distant place is **produced** by computers. The computers can also create settings from long ago.

People on a Virtual Vacation feel as if they are really visiting a place. They can do all the things that they would do if they were really there. In fact, they never leave the Virtual Vacation Room.

"Just yell when you want to come home," said Jill. "I'll be at the controls."

**Stop   Think   Write**

VOCABULARY

In the story, images are produced by computers. What is a synonym for **produced**?

_____

_____

_____

Suddenly, the Ortizes were staring at a strange being with two heads. It was sleeping on a couch. "This isn't very exciting," said Mrs. Ortiz. "I don't see any volcanoes."

Like their parents, the Ortiz children were not **impressed** by the snoring being with two heads. "Where are all the fun rides?" they asked.

The Ortizes could see that they were not at Volcano Vacationland. They yelled for Jill to bring them back.

**Stop** **Think** **Write**

STORY STRUCTURE

**What happens first to the Ortizes in the Virtual Vacation Room?**

_____

_____

_____

"I must have pushed the wrong button," **admitted** Jill. "I think I sent you to the planet Frufee by mistake." The Ortizes decided to try again.

Soon they heard what sounded like gunfire. Suddenly, a soldier was shouting at them. "This can't be right," said Mr. Ortiz. "It looks more like the American Revolution."

They yelled again for Jill to bring them back.

"I'm sorry," she said. "I must have pushed the buttons for a battle in 1781."

**Stop** **Think** **Write**

STORY STRUCTURE

How would you describe Jill?

_____

_____

_____

"I promise to get it right this time," said Jill. She carefully pushed the buttons.

The Ortizes huddled together in **suspense**. Each of them wondered what would happen this time. Would they meet another weird being? Would they find themselves in the middle of a battle?

Then a strange landscape came into view.

**Stop** **Think** **Write**

VOCABULARY

**Why do you think the Ortizes huddled together in <u>suspense</u>?**

_____

_____

_____

**169**

The Ortizes saw volcanoes. They saw fun rides. They saw swimming pools surrounded by hot lava. They even seemed to be riding in a car.

"Hurray!" yelled the Ortizes. "We're finally at Volcano Vacationland."

"It seems that Jill has pushed the right buttons," said Mrs. Ortiz.

Of course, the Ortizes were just standing in the Virtual Vacation Room. They had forgotten that. They were on their fun vacation at last.

**Stop** | **Think** | **Write**

STORY STRUCTURE

**Where does the end of the story take place?**

_____

_____

_____

## Look Back and Respond

**1** **What settings are there in the story?**

_____

_____

_____

**Hint**

You can find clues on almost every page.

**2** **What happens to the Ortizes the first two times they try to go on their vacation?**

_____

_____

_____

**Hint**

For clues, see pages 167 and 168.

**3** **How are the Ortizes finally able to visit Volcano Vacationland?**

_____

_____

_____

**Hint**

For clues, see pages 169 and 170.

**4** **If you could go on a Virtual Vacation, where would you go? Why?**

_____

_____

_____

**Hint**

Part of your answer to question 1 and details in the story should help you.

# Be a Reading Detective!

Return to

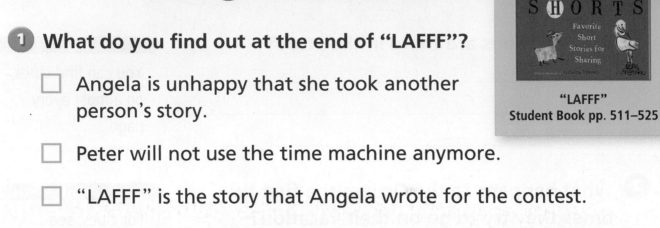

**"LAFFF"**
Student Book pp. 511–525

**1** **What do you find out at the end of "LAFFF"?**

☐ Angela is unhappy that she took another person's story.

☐ Peter will not use the time machine anymore.

☐ "LAFFF" is the story that Angela wrote for the contest.

**Prove It!** What evidence in the story supports your answer?
Check the boxes. ☑ Make notes.

| Evidence | Notes |
|---|---|
| ☐ what Peter says after she wins | |
| ☐ what Angela thinks and says at the end | |
| ☐ what Angela reads at the end | |
| ☐ how Angela's story starts | |

**Write About It!**

STORY STRUCTURE

Answer question **1** using evidence from the text.

_____

_____

_____

_____

_____

_____

_____

**2** **What can you conclude about Angela?**

☐ She wants to win, but she is honest.

☐ She wants to win no matter what it takes.

☐ She doesn't care if she does well in school.

**Prove It!** What evidence in the story supports your answer?
Check the boxes. ☑ Make notes.

| Evidence | Notes |
|---|---|
| ☐ how Angela feels right after the contest | |
| ☐ how Angela feels at the end of the story | |
| ☐ what Peter says at the end of the story | |
| ☐ | |

**Write About It!**

CONCLUSIONS AND GENERALIZATIONS

Answer question **2** using evidence from the text.

_____

_____

_____

_____

_____

_____

**background**
**career**
**formula**
**insights**
**required**

# Magazine Writers

**1** If you want to write for magazines, here's something you should know. Many skills are **required**. You must write in a clear and interesting way. You must find ways to draw in your readers.

**When you write an essay, what skills are required?**

_____

_____

_____

**2** Building a **career** as a magazine writer can be tough. Most writers have to start at the bottom. They slowly work their way up.

**What career interests you? Explain.**

_____

_____

_____

**3** Writers can get **insights** into a subject by experiencing it for themselves. A story about skydiving is more interesting if the writer has actually jumped from a plane.

**How might working for a vet give a person insights about animals?**

_____

_____

_____

**4** The **formula** for a great magazine story is to put together a good idea, good research, and good writing.

**What is the formula for a great party?**

_____

_____

_____

**5** Many newspapers and magazines are now published on the Internet as well as on paper. Most writers today have some **background** in using computers.

**Write a synonym for background.**

_____

# Making a Magazine

by Dolores Vasquez

What does it take to make a magazine? Our class was getting ready to find out. We had decided to plan and publish our own magazine.

First, we would learn everything that's **required** to make a magazine. We'd need to choose story ideas. Then we'd do research and gather facts. We'd write stories and take photographs to go with them.

To get started, we looked at other magazines for ideas. We read the stories. We studied the pictures. We began to discuss plans for our own magazine. What sort of articles should be in the magazine? How should it look?

| Stop | Think | Write |

VOCABULARY

How does the class learn what is <u>required</u> to make a magazine?

_____

_____

_____

## Learning from an Expert

"Students," said Mr. Gomez, "I'd like to introduce the best magazine writer in the nation. This is Annie Smith. She travels around the world writing about exciting events. Still, when she first started work, she was closer to home."

Annie told us about her first job. She worked at a magazine in the small town where she grew up. She wrote about interesting people who lived there. Her favorite story was about an old man who ran a bakery. People came from far away to buy his cakes, but they did not know his **background**. He had once worked as a chef at the White House!

Annie's story about the old man won a prize. That really helped her **career** take off.

### Stop | Think | Write

FACT AND OPINION

When Mr. Gomez calls Annie the best magazine writer in the nation, is he stating a fact or an opinion? Explain.

_____

_____

_____

**175**

## Planning Stories

Annie gave us many **insights** into what makes a good magazine story. Now it was time for us to come up with our own story ideas. We decided to follow Annie's **formula**. We'd interview interesting people in our own neighborhood.

We talked about people who lived and worked nearby. Everyone suggested ideas. Then we chose our favorites. We picked three people to interview.

The class split up into three teams of writers. Each would interview one person and write a story.

**Stop** **Think** **Write**

VOCABULARY

What is Annie's <u>formula</u>? How does it help the students choose what to write about?

_____

_____

_____

176

My team had come up with a great idea for the magazine. Although we lived in the city, we would write about activities that usually take place in the country.

Shana knew a family who lived near the park. They kept bees. Paul had an uncle who raised chickens.

"Nobody is interested in chickens," said Shana.

"Any subject can be interesting if the writer makes it interesting," said Mr. Gomez. Then he reminded us about the community garden that many of us passed each day on the way to school. How could we find out who had started it? What did people grow there?

"That's a great idea, Mr. G," I said.

## Stop   Think   Write

FACT AND OPINION

**Which statements on this page are opinions? Explain.**

_____

_____

_____

## Conducting an Interview

My team went to the community garden. We asked around and found that it was started by a woman named Laura Antonio. We searched her out. She told us that the garden used to be an empty lot. Now twenty different families grew food there. Laura grew enough tomatoes to make ten gallons of tomato sauce each summer!

We asked Laura about her background. How did she learn how to grow things? Laura explained that she grew up on a farm in Italy. When she moved to the United States, she missed growing things. She decided to start the community garden. She helped other city families grow vegetables there, too.

**Stop   Think   Write**

CAUSE AND EFFECT

**Why did Laura start the community garden?**

_____

_____

_____

## Putting It All Together

The interview with Laura gave us great insights into how a community garden works. We learned why gardens are great for the community.

There was still more work to do. We did research in the library and on the Internet. We learned more facts about community gardens to add to our story. Then we wrote the story. We checked to make sure all the information was correct. Finally, we reread the story and made a few changes to improve it.

We had a lot of photographs, and we couldn't decide which ones to use. So, we showed them to another team. Together, we worked out which ones were best.

**Stop** | **Think** | **Write**

CAUSE AND EFFECT

**Why do the writers show their photographs to another team?**

_____

_____

_____

## Publishing the Magazine

At last, we had all finished our stories. Nobody has ever worked so hard! We were ready to put our words and photographs together on the computer. When we were finished, we printed out one copy of the new magazine. We checked it to make sure there were no mistakes. There were mistakes! We fixed them. Then we printed out lots of copies for our friends, families, and other students at school.

We had published our first magazine! We learned a lot and had fun, too. Maybe some of us will be famous magazine writers some day!

**Stop** | **Think** | **Write**

CAUSE AND EFFECT

**Why do the students print out just one copy of their magazine at first?**

_____

_____

_____

# Look Back and Respond

**1** What great idea do the students have for their magazine?

_____

_____

_____

**Hint**

For clues, see page 177.

**2** What insights about community gardens might Laura give that wouldn't be found in books?

_____

_____

_____

**Hint**

For clues, see pages 178 and 179.

**3** Why does the team do more research after they have interviewed Laura?

_____

_____

_____

**Hint**

For clues, see page 179.

**4** On page 180, the narrator says, "There were mistakes!" Is the statement a fact or an opinion? Explain.

_____

_____

_____

**Hint**

Think about the differences between facts and opinions.

# Be a Reading Detective!

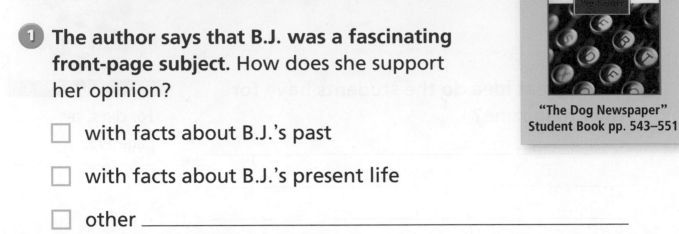

**Return to**

"The Dog Newspaper"
Student Book pp. 543–551

**1** **The author says that B.J. was a fascinating front-page subject.** How does she support her opinion?

☐ with facts about B.J.'s past

☐ with facts about B.J.'s present life

☐ other _____

**Prove It!** What evidence in the selection supports your answer? Check the boxes. ☑ Make notes.

| Evidence | Notes |
|---|---|
| ☐ details about B.J. during the war | |
| ☐ details about B.J.'s trip to the U.S. | |
| ☐ | |

**Write About It!**

FACT AND OPINION

Answer question **1** using evidence from the text.

_____
_____
_____
_____
_____
_____
_____

**2** In what way is B.J. like the other neighborhood dogs?

☐ All of the dogs have interesting pasts.

☐ He sleeps in a gingerbread house.

☐ Most of what he does isn't very interesting.

**Prove It!** What evidence in the selection supports your answer? Check the boxes. ☑ Make notes.

| Evidence | Notes |
|---|---|
| ☐ details of B.J.'s activities | |
| ☐ what others say about their dogs | |
| ☐ | |

**Write About It!**

COMPARE AND CONTRAST

Answer question **2** using evidence from the text.

_____

_____

_____

_____

_____

_____

**Lesson**

# 19

✓ **TARGET VOCABULARY**

dependent
effective
exception
issue
urge

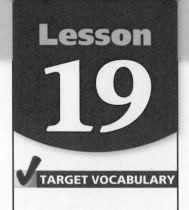

# The Fight for Equal Rights

## Rights for Enslaved People

Enslaved people did not have control over their own lives. They were bought and sold. Their owners could mistreat them.

Some people wanted to end slavery and give enslaved people rights. Others wanted slavery to continue. For years, the two sides argued over the ❶ _____ of slavery.

# Rights for Women

Women had few rights in the 1800s. They could not even vote. Many women began to

**2** _____ Congress to give them the vote.

Before 1900, almost all women were

**3** _____ on husbands or fathers. Later, laws gave women more rights. Then women proved that they could take care of themselves.

Few women worked outside the home in the 1800s. One **4** _____ was Elizabeth Blackwell. In the 1850s, she became a doctor.

# A Fighter for All People's Rights

Sojourner Truth fought for equal rights. She was an **5** _____ speaker. She connected with her audience. Her strong words moved many people to act.

# Sojourner Truth

## Speaker for Equal Rights
### by Duncan Searl

## Her Early Life

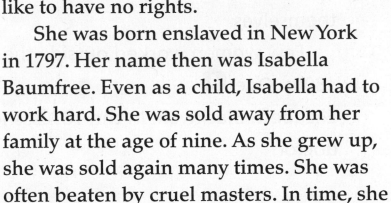

Sojourner Truth fought for equal rights for all people. She did this because she knew what it was like to have no rights.

She was born enslaved in New York in 1797. Her name then was Isabella Baumfree. Even as a child, Isabella had to work hard. She was sold away from her family at the age of nine. As she grew up, she was sold again many times. She was often beaten by cruel masters. In time, she married and had five children. Several of her children were sold.

**Stop** **Think** **Write**

UNDERSTANDING CHARACTERS

**Why were equal rights so important to Isabella Baumfree? Explain, using details the author provides.**

_____

_____

_____

# Isabella Finds Freedom and Strength

By the 1800s, many states had passed laws against slavery. New York's enslaved people became free in 1827. Isabella Baumfree's owner promised to free her. He went back on his promise, so Isabella escaped to freedom. She took her baby, Sophia, with her.

A kind couple took Isabella in. With their help, she went to court to get her son Peter back. He had been sold to a slave owner in the South. It took a year for Isabella to win her case. At last she got her son back!

## Stop | Think | Write

AUTHOR'S PURPOSE

It took Baumfree a year to win her case and get her son back. Why do you think the author includes this information?

_____

_____

_____

185

# Isabella Becomes Sojourner Truth

Freed from slavery, Isabella felt like a new person. Her hard early life made her want to help others. To do that, she gave speeches. In her speeches, she shared her beliefs.

Isabella was an **effective** speaker. People listened closely. Her words gave them courage and hope. She never made much money. For food, she was often **dependent** on the kindness of others.

In 1843, she changed her name. She became Sojourner Truth. A sojourner is a traveler. Sojourner Truth felt that this new name showed what she wanted to do with her life.

**Stop · Think · Write**

What does the author say to convince readers that Baumfree was an <u>effective</u> speaker?

_____

_____

_____

# Sojourner Truth, Abolitionist

At that time, many people were trying to end slavery. These people were called abolitionists. Sojourner Truth joined the abolitionist cause. She knew that her words against slavery would have great meaning. After all, she had been enslaved. She gave speeches on this issue.

Sojourner Truth met other abolitionists. One was Frederick Douglass. He had also escaped slavery. Douglass was one of the great abolitionist speakers.

In 1850, Sojourner Truth published her life story. She had never learned to write. She couldn't even read. So a friend wrote down her words.

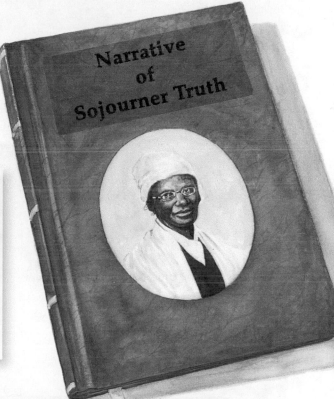

Frederick Douglass spoke out against slavery.

## Stop | Think | Write

CAUSE AND EFFECT

**Sojourner Truth and Frederick Douglass both escaped slavery. How do you think this helped them as abolitionist speakers?**

_____

_____

_____

# Women Deserve Rights, Too

Many abolitionists were women. However, women had few rights themselves. Only men could vote. There was no **exception** to that rule. Only men could hold most jobs. Many people thought that women were too weak to work.

Not Sojourner Truth! She knew how hard women could work. She began to **urge** women to claim their rights. In 1851, she spoke at the Women's Rights Convention in Akron, Ohio.

"Look at my arm!" she cried in her huge voice. "I have plowed and planted and gathered into barns." She added, "I could work as much and eat as much as a man—when I could get it." For the rest of her life, she kept speaking out.

**Stop** | **Think** | **Write**

VOCABULARY

Why did Sojourner Truth <u>urge</u> women to gain their rights?

_____

_____

_____

# After Slavery Ended

In time, one of Sojourner Truth's dreams came true. Slavery was ended in the U.S. in 1865. Sojourner Truth kept working to help African Americans. She helped ex-slaves settle in the West. She tried to get land grants for many of them.

She did not see women gain the right to vote. That did not happen until 1920. Sojourner Truth died in 1883. She was 86. A strong, brave woman, Truth spent her life helping others.

**Stop** **Think** **Write**

AUTHOR'S PURPOSE

**Why did the author include details about the work Sojourner Truth did after slavery ended?**

_____

_____

_____

# Did You Know?

- ◎ Sojourner Truth grew up speaking Dutch. She did not learn English until she was nine.

- ◎ By the time Sojourner Truth was 13, she had been sold three times.

- ◎ In the early 1850s, Sojourner Truth journeyed through 22 states. Everywhere she went, she spoke against slavery.

- ◎ Sojourner Truth was six feet tall and very strong. She wasn't afraid of angry crowds!

- ◎ Sojourner Truth met Abraham Lincoln in 1864. They had a long talk.

**Stop** | **Think** | **Write**

UNDERSTANDING CHARACTERS

**How do these facts help you know Sojourner Truth better?**

_____

_____

_____

# Look Back and Respond

**1** What issues were important to Sojourner Truth?

_____

_____

_____

**Hint**

For clues, see pages 184, 187, and 188.

**2** What point does the author make about the life of Sojourner Truth? What evidence does he provide?

_____

_____

_____

**Hint**

Clues are on every page!

**3** What words would you use to describe Sojourner Truth?

_____

_____

_____

**Hint**

Your answers to questions 1 and 2 should help you.

**4** In what ways do people like Sojourner Truth help make our world better?

_____

_____

_____

**Hint**

Your answer to question 3 should help you.

# Be a Reading Detective!

Return to

"Darnell Rock Reporting"
Student Book pp. 569–581

**1** **Why do you think the author wrote this story?**

☐ to tell an interesting story

☐ to explain how to start a community garden

☐ to persuade people to take action

**Prove It!** What evidence in the story supports your answer? Check the boxes. ☑ Make notes.

| Evidence | Notes |
|---|---|
| ☐ what Sweeby Jones says | |
| ☐ what Darnell says at the meeting | |
| ☐ what happens after the meeting | |

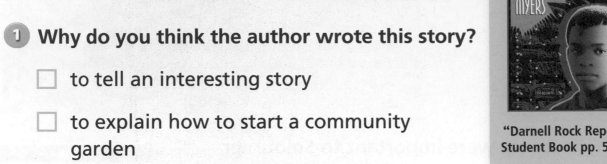

## Write About It!

AUTHOR'S PURPOSE

Answer question **1** using evidence from the text.

_____

_____

_____

_____

_____

_____

_____

**2** **Did Darnell's article do any good?**

☐ Yes, it led to important changes.

☐ No, nothing changed.

☐ other _____

**Prove It!** What evidence in the story supports your answer? Check the boxes. ☑ Make notes.

| Evidence | Notes |
|---|---|
| ☐ what someone wants to donate | |
| ☐ what the paper wants Darnell to do | |
| ☐ | |

**Write About It!**

Answer question **2** using evidence from the text.

_____

_____

_____

_____

_____

_____

_____

**In the Wild**

**descended**
**diminishing**
**marveling**
**quivered**
**rhythmic**

**1** Rob stood on a hilltop and looked at the trees and the lake. Then he **descended** to the valley.

As Rob <u>descended</u>, was he on flat land or sloping land?

_____

**2** Rob heard a loud, **rhythmic** tapping above him. It was a woodpecker on a tree.

What is another sound that can have a regular, <u>rhythmic</u> pattern?

_____

**3** He stood still, **marveling** at how quiet the valley was. There were no car horns, no music players, no machine sounds at all.

Name a place you really want to visit. What would you be <u>marveling</u> at in that place?

_____

_____

_____

**4** Suddenly, a hare bounded out of the underbrush. It stood still and looked at Rob. Its shiny brown fur **quivered** a bit. Was it cold, or was it afraid of this large, strange human?

**How could Rob tell that the hare quivered?**

_____

_____

_____

**5** The clouds grew thick and dark for a moment, and the wind rose. But then the sun broke through again. Rob's worry about the weather was **diminishing**. He decided that a storm was not coming after all. He would stay here awhile.

**What is one sign that a storm is diminishing in strength?**

_____

_____

_____

# Horse Rider

## by Judy Rosenbaum

The bus ride had already lasted an hour. No wonder the people at the Community Center had asked Celia Rivera and her mother to travel with Mrs. Grant and her granddaughter, Daisy. The Grants were new in Williston. They never would have found the Sunflower Stables on their own.

As Celia's mom chatted with Mrs. Grant, Daisy just stared out the window. Daisy's nervous expression made Celia wonder if that girl ever went outside at all. Mom had explained that Mrs. Grant was homeschooling Daisy for now. "Daisy is still feeling the effects of a very bad event," Mom had told Celia. "We hope that the people at Sunflower Stables can help set her free."

Celia was glad that she and Mom could also help, even if it was just a little bit.

---

### Stop | Think | Write

UNDERSTANDING CHARACTERS

How would you describe Celia? How do her thoughts or actions support your ideas?

_____

_____

_____

The bus stopped at last. The Riveras and the Grants **descended** the steps. Mom checked her map to see where they had to walk. After ten minutes, they reached the stables.

Inside the grounds were several fenced-in rings. In one, a woman was leading a horse with a boy riding it. A man walked alongside. He held onto the boy. Celia's eyes widened. Wow, horses were huge! The boy looked happy. Outside the ring stood an empty wheelchair.

Mom had explained that spending time on horseback often helped people with some kinds of disabilities. But how could a large animal help a scared kid like Daisy?

**Stop** **Think** **Write**

VOCABULARY

When the Riveras and the Grants <u>descended</u> the steps, did they go up or down?

_____

_____

_____

Daisy didn't have a physical challenge. Mentally, however, she had not yet recovered from a tornado in her old town. She had been trapped in the ruins of a shopping mall for hours. Daisy still had nightmares. Even now, she almost never spoke. The family had moved from their old town to Williston. But nothing had helped Daisy.

A woman came over to them. She said, "Hello, Daisy. I'm your side walker, Margie. When you're riding on your horse, I'll hold onto you."

Daisy didn't say a word. A man led a horse out of the barn, and Daisy's hand **quivered** as she reached for her grandmother. Even Celia backed up when the large, large horse got close.

**Stop** | **Think** | **Write**

What is the main problem in the story?

_____

_____

_____

"This is Rudy," said Margie, introducing the man. "He's one of our riding teachers." The man smiled and shook hands with Mom and Mrs. Grant.

"And this is Comet," said the man, introducing the horse. "She's an eight-year-old mare."

Comet's large, brown head seemed to loom over Celia. The horse's eyes were huge. Her mouth was huge. Her teeth were probably huge, too. Her neck and chest seemed to be made of muscles. Celia was sure that at any moment, the horse would rear up on her back legs. Then she would be ten feet tall—at least! "Oh, why did I have to think of that?" Celia said to herself.

**Stop** **Think** **Write**

UNDERSTANDING CHARACTERS

How does Celia feel when the horse is brought over? How can you tell?

_____

_____

_____

197

"Don't worry, Comet is gentle," said Rudy. "Look how velvety her nose is. Would you like to touch it, Daisy?" Rudy held Comet's head steady and showed Daisy how to touch a horse's nose. Daisy didn't say anything, but to Celia's surprise, Daisy did reach out cautiously and stroke the bridge of that big nose. Celia found herself reaching for Comet's nose, too. It did feel like velvet. She felt her own fear **diminishing**.

Then Rudy showed how smoothly the horse walked. Comet's hooves made a **rhythmic** sound on the hard earth.

Margie turned to Celia and said, "How would you like to show Daisy how to sit on a horse?"

## Stop · Think · Write

If Celia's fear is **diminishing**, is it becoming greater or less?

_____

_____

_____

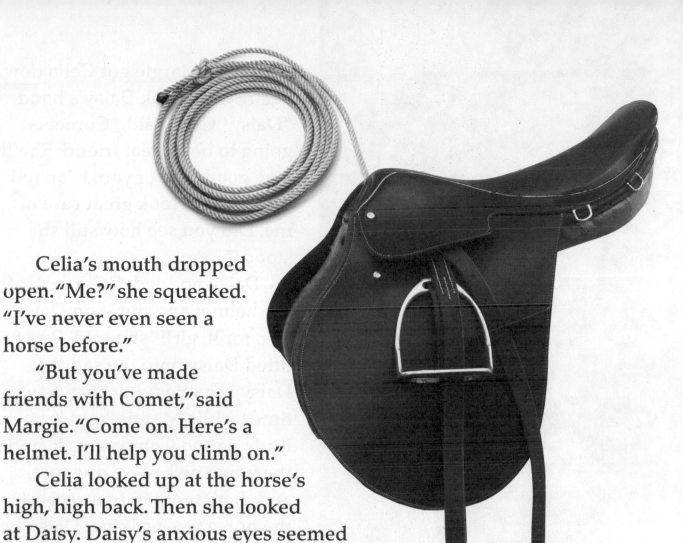

Celia's mouth dropped open. "Me?" she squeaked. "I've never even seen a horse before."

"But you've made friends with Comet," said Margie. "Come on. Here's a helmet. I'll help you climb on."

Celia looked up at the horse's high, high back. Then she looked at Daisy. Daisy's anxious eyes seemed almost as large as Comet's. This kid deserved to feel better about life. Celia took a deep breath and said, "Okay. How do I climb up there?"

With a lot of help from Rudy, Celia still wasn't exactly sure how she ended up on Comet's back. To her surprise, the saddle was pretty comfortable. She looked down, **marveling** at how still the horse was. "Hey, Daisy, it's fun up here!" she said. It was fun.

### Stop | Think | Write

UNDERSTANDING CHARACTERS

**What do you know about Celia at this point in the story? What does she think, say, or do that helps you know?**

_____

_____

_____

When Margie got Celia down again, Celia took Daisy's hand. "Daisy," Celia said, "Comet is going to be a great friend. She'll take good care of you. I can tell because she took great care of me. Did you see how still she stood?"

Daisy nodded. Celia took off the helmet and put it on Daisy. "Go for it, girl!" she said. Rudy lifted Daisy onto the saddle. Daisy breathed quickly a few times while Margie held her. Rudy patted Comet's neck, and the horse picked up one foot, and then another. In a second, the horse was walking. Daisy looked down from the saddle.

"Cool!" she said.

**Stop | Think | Write**

STORY STRUCTURE

What does the last line of the story tell you? What has changed?

_____

_____

_____

## Look Back and Respond

**1** Why were Celia and her mother asked to travel with the Grants?

**Hint**
For clues, see page 194.

_____

_____

_____

**2** What problem almost gets in the way of Celia's being able to help Daisy?

**Hint**
For clues, see pages 195, 197, and 199.

_____

_____

_____

**3** What effect does Celia's brave act have on Daisy?

**Hint**
For clues, see pages 199 and 200.

_____

_____

_____

**4** Do you think the author believes that animals can help people feel better? Use details from the story to support your answer.

**Hint**
You can find clues on almost every page.

_____

_____

_____

# Be a Reading Detective!

Return to

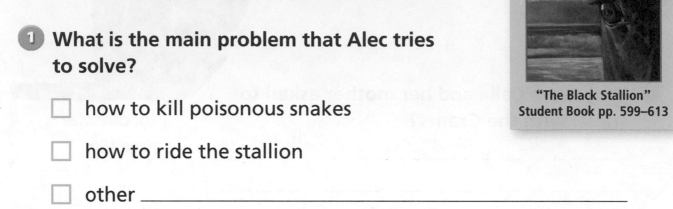

"The Black Stallion"
Student Book pp. 599–613

**1** **What is the main problem that Alec tries to solve?**

☐ how to kill poisonous snakes

☐ how to ride the stallion

☐ other _____

**Prove It!** What evidence in the story supports your answer?
Check the boxes. ☑ Make notes.

| Evidence | Notes |
|---|---|
| ☐ what Alec does after the stallion kills the snake | |
| ☐ details about Alec talking to the stallion | |
| ☐ | |

## Write About It!

STORY STRUCTURE

**Answer question 1 using evidence from the text.**

_____

_____

_____

_____

_____

_____

_____

**2** **What do Alec's actions tell you about him?**

☐ He will keep trying until he reaches his goal.

☐ He spends most of his time feeling sorry for himself.

☐ other _____

**Prove It!** What evidence in the story supports your answer?
Check the boxes. ☑ Make notes.

| Evidence | Notes |
|---|---|
| ☐ what he does after being thrown | |
| ☐ how he learns to be a better rider | |
| ☐ | |

**Write About It!**

CONCLUSIONS AND GENERALIZATIONS

**Answer question 2 using evidence from the text.**

_____

_____

_____

_____

_____

_____

_____

**201B**

✓ **TARGET VOCABULARY**

evident
factor
pace
salvation
undoubtedly

# The Gold Rush

In 1848, gold was discovered in California. It was **evident** that there was plenty more to be found. Many people decided to go there to get rich.

More than 300,000 people were part of the Gold Rush. They traveled by sea or by covered wagon. Either way, the **pace** of the trip was very slow.

Many of these travelers arrived in 1849. They became known as forty-niners. They hoped the gold would be their **salvation**.

The Gold Rush was a main **factor** in California's growth. In one year, the population of San Francisco grew from 1,000 to 25,000.

The Gold Rush was important in the history of California. It was **undoubtedly** bad for the environment. It was also bad for the American Indians. They were pushed off their land.

**1** The forty-niners hoped the gold would be their
_____.

**2** One major _____ in
California's growth was the Gold Rush.

**3** The _____ was very slow
for people who traveled by sea or by covered
wagon.

**4** What are some facts about your school that
are <u>undoubtedly</u> true?

_____

_____

_____

**5** What weather conditions might make it
<u>evident</u> that a storm is on its way?

_____

_____

_____

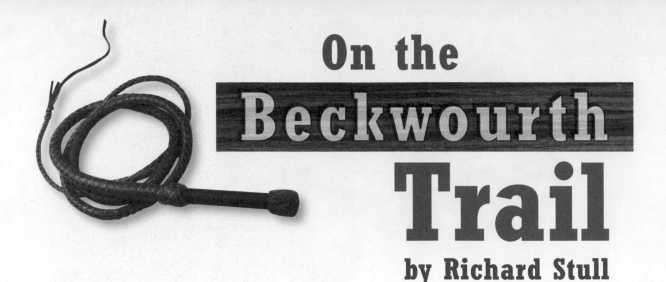

# On the Beckwourth Trail

## by Richard Stull

James Beckwourth stood looking out over the land. Before him lay the Sierra Nevada Mountains. California lay on the other side. His job was to lead a wagon train through the mountains.

The year was 1851. The travelers were part of the California Gold Rush. They all hoped to find gold and become rich. They had hired James to guide them.

James knew the way. In fact, he had discovered the trail through the mountains. James also knew that the travelers **undoubtedly** needed a guide. Without one, they were sure to get lost.

| Stop | Think | Write |
|------|-------|-------|

VOCABULARY

**Why do the travelers undoubtedly need a guide?**

_____

_____

_____

That night, James met with the men and women of the wagon train. He first showed them a map he had drawn. "We must keep a steady **pace** on our trip," he said. "Doing so will help us cross the mountains before the first snows hit."

"What other things should we do on the trip?" asked one man. James told them to avoid wild animals such as bears. He told them to keep the children close to the wagons at all times. He also told them not to waste their drinking water. It was **evident** to the travelers that James was an experienced mountain man.

## Stop | Think | Write

SEQUENCE OF EVENTS

**What is the first thing that James does at the meeting with the travelers?**

_____

_____

_____

The trip proved to be difficult, and the days turned into weeks. The travelers knew that the weather would be a huge **factor** in the success of the journey. They also knew that the first snow would soon fall. Even James began to worry. He decided to have another meeting with the travelers.

"I need to ride ahead," James said. "I will be able to tell how many days we have left before we leave the mountains."

The people looked at one another. They were not sure that they could trust James to return for them. They decided to vote on if he should go or stay.

**Stop** **Think** **Write**

CAUSE AND EFFECT

Why would the weather be important in the success of the journey?

_____

_____

_____

The travelers decided to let James ride ahead. The next morning, he mounted his horse and rode off. Before he left, he urged the people to keep moving as fast as possible. He told them that he would be back within a week.

The wagon train plodded along. The September nights grew colder and colder. Five days after James left, a woman thought she saw him in the distance. "James has returned," she yelled. As the wagons rolled closer, the people saw that it was an American Indian chief, watching them from afar.

**Stop** | **Think** | **Write**

SEQUENCE OF EVENTS

**What does James do just before he rides off?**

_____

_____

_____

On the night of the seventh day, the people gathered around their campfires. They were worried that James might not return. They were also worried about the American Indian they had seen. Maybe he was not friendly. Maybe he would return with other warriors.

Suddenly, they heard the sound of a horse traveling fast over the land. Everyone stood up to listen. The adults hid the children in the wagons.

Just then, James rode into the light of the campfires. He hopped down from his horse. "I'm starving," he said. "What's for dinner?"

**Stop** | **Think** | **Write**

SEQUENCE OF EVENTS

**What happens just before James tells the travelers that he is hungry?**

_____

_____

_____

The men and women crowded around James. "How close are we to Marysville?" asked one woman. Marysville was an important and growing city. It was located right in the middle of the area where people were finding gold.

"We're about a week's journey away," explained James. "We're a lot closer than I thought we were."

The people shouted with joy. They knew that they had made it through the mountains in time. They also knew that their brave guide James Beckwourth had been their **salvation**.

**Stop** **Think** **Write**

VOCABULARY

**Why do the travelers think of James Beckwourth as their <u>salvation</u>?**

_____

_____

_____

## California Gold Rush

Thousands of people used the Beckwourth Trail during the Gold Rush. The Gold Rush began in 1848 and lasted about 10 years.

## The Beckwourth Trail

James opened his wagon trail in 1851. People used the trail to cross the mountains to Marysville.

## Marysville, California

The city of Marysville promised to pay James for improving the trail. More people in the city meant more money for everyone. The city did not pay him.

## In Thanks

Marysville gave its largest park a new name in 1996. The park is now called Beckwourth Riverfront Park. It honors James Beckwourth.

**Stop** **Think** **Write**

SEQUENCE OF EVENTS

How soon after the beginning of the Gold Rush does James Beckwourth open the trail?

_____

_____

# Look Back and Respond

**1** What is James Beckwourth's role as the wagon train's guide?

_____

_____

_____

**Hint**

For clues, see pages 204 and 205.

**2** What important event occurs during the second meeting between James and the travelers?

_____

_____

_____

**Hint**

For clues, see pages 206 and 207.

**3** How would you describe James Beckwourth's character?

_____

_____

_____

**Hint**

You can find clues on almost every page.

**4** Do you think the people of Marysville, California, realize what they owe to James Beckwourth? What makes you think the way you do?

_____

_____

_____

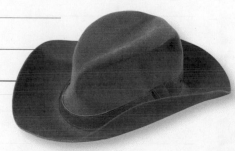

**Hint**

For clues, see page 210.

# Be a Reading Detective!

Return to

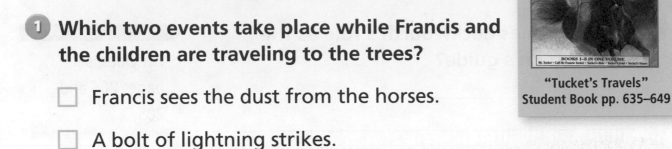

"Tucket's Travels"
Student Book pp. 635–649

**1** **Which two events take place while Francis and the children are traveling to the trees?**

☐ Francis sees the dust from the horses.

☐ A bolt of lightning strikes.

☐ Francis stops brushing away their tracks.

**Prove It!** What evidence in the story supports your answer? Check the boxes. ✓ Make notes.

| Evidence | Notes |
|---|---|
| ☐ the plume of dust Francis sees | |
| ☐ details as they hurry toward the trees | |
| ☐ the illustrations | |

## Write About It!

SEQUENCE OF EVENTS

Answer question **1** using evidence from the text.

_____

_____

_____

_____

_____

_____

_____

_____

**2** Which word describes Francis?

☐ panicky     ☐ responsible

☐ bored     ☐ selfish

**Prove It!** What evidence in the story supports your answer?
Check the boxes. ☑ Make notes.

| Evidence | Notes |
|---|---|
| ☐ how Francis stays with Lottie and Billy | |
| ☐ how Francis tries to keep them safe | |
| ☐ | |

**Write About It!**

UNDERSTANDING CHARACTERS

Answer question **2** using evidence from the text.

_____

_____

_____

_____

_____

_____

_____

✓ **TARGET VOCABULARY**

**astonished**
**deserted**
**margins**
**reasoned**
**spared**

# The Plains Indians

**1** The Spanish brought horses to the Plains in the 1500s. The American Indians of the Plains were **astonished** when they first saw these animals.

**What sight have you seen that <u>astonished</u> you? Explain.**

_____

_____

_____

**2** Plains Indians moved often. After living for a time in one place, they **deserted** it. They moved somewhere else, where the hunting was better. This was a difficult thing to do on foot.

**Write a synonym for <u>deserted</u>.**

_____

**3** Most Plains tribes built their tepees along the **margins** of rivers and streams. At the edges of these waterways, water for cooking and washing was plentiful.

**What are some things you might find today along the margins of a river?**

_____

_____

_____

**4** "If we tame and raise horses," the Plains Indians **reasoned**, "our lives will get better. Then we can move about freely to follow the buffalo herds. We can hunt on horseback, too."

**Tell about a time that you reasoned out a solution to a problem.**

_____

_____

_____

**5** Horses **spared** the Plains Indians from much hardship. They no longer had to walk long distances. They could hunt for food more easily on horseback.

**Has a friend or relative ever spared you from a hardship or difficulty? Tell about it.**

_____

_____

_____

# Orphan Boy and the Elk Dogs

by Duncan Searl

No one knew where Orphan Boy had come from. His clothes were rags, and he ate scraps that no one wanted. The children in the village would not play with him. The grown-ups did not trust him or want him in their tepees. So Orphan Boy lived in the bushes at the **margins** of the village.

At night, Orphan Boy edged closer to the campfires. One old woman was sometimes kind to him. She gave the hungry boy food and sometimes let him sit near her fire.

## Stop Think Write

VOCABULARY

**Why does Orphan Boy live at the margins of the village?**

_____

_____

_____

One night, the woman told Orphan Boy about the Elk Dogs. "Far away to the south," she explained, "the people live under a giant lake. These people keep animals that are as big as Elk and as loyal and as hardworking as Dog!"

Orphan Boy was **astonished**. How could people live under a lake? Could there really be an animal as big as Elk and as hardworking as Dog?

"If we had Elk Dogs," the woman said, "our people would be strong and free." Then she added sadly, "Our greatest hunters have traveled to this lake to get the Elk Dogs, but they have never returned."

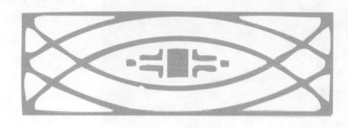

## Stop | Think | Write

INFER AND PREDICT

**Why do you think the greatest hunters tried to get the Elk Dogs for the village?**

_____

_____

_____

That night, Orphan Boy made a decision. He would get Elk Dogs for the village. At dawn, he set out.

For thirty days, Orphan Boy walked steadily south. He crossed high mountains and cold, deep rivers. He walked until his feet bled. Hungry, lonely, and exhausted, he finally came to a lake.

"You're late!" said a voice. Orphan Boy spun around. A kingfisher was talking to him! "Come with me," the big bird urged. "Grandfather is waiting!" Then it dove into the lake and disappeared.

**Stop** | **Think** | **Write**

THEME

**What personal traits does Orphan Boy show as he goes about his difficult task?**

_____

_____

_____

216

Orphan Boy stared at the cold lake water. Should he follow the talking bird? "If I do," the boy **reasoned**, "I might disappear like the other hunters who came for the Elk Dogs."

Putting aside his fears, Orphan Boy dove into the dark water. He did not even get wet! Somehow the water moved away, and he found himself in front of a giant tepee.

The kingfisher sat on top of the tepee. "Enter Grandfather's tepee," the bird said.

Inside, the tepee was warm and dark. At one end sat the old grandfather. He wore a long, dark robe, and his white hair fell to his shoulders.

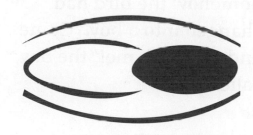

**Stop** **Think** **Write**

STORY STRUCTURE

**What magical help does Orphan Boy get on his unusual journey?**

_____

_____

_____

**217**

Pots of food suddenly appeared on the floor, and Orphan Boy ate hungrily. "You are different from the others who tried to come here," the grandfather told him. "At the lake, they became afraid and **deserted**. You, however, were brave enough to dive into the water. Because you are brave, your life will be **spared**."

Just then, Orphan Boy saw two Elk Dogs through the open tepee door. One was as black as night; the other was brown with snow-white spots. Tall and sleek, they raced through the golden grass.

Orphan Boy also saw the kingfisher outside. Somehow the bird had changed into a boy. "Come and ride with me!" the boy called.

**Stop | Think | Write**

VOCABULARY

**Why is Orphan Boy's life <u>spared</u>?**

_____

_____

_____

The two boys climbed onto Elk Dogs and galloped down the valley. They rode for hours. Later, as they rested, Orphan Boy said, "I want to bring some Elk Dogs home with me."

"Grandfather will not just give them to you," the kingfisher boy warned. "However, if you find out his secret, he will give you any gift you want. Try to see his feet under his long robe. Then you will know his secret."

For six days, Orphan Boy stayed in the grandfather's tepee. He never saw the old man's feet. The long black robe always covered them. Finally, it was time for Orphan Boy to leave the mysterious land under the lake.

**Stop** **Think** **Write**

STORY STRUCTURE

**What final task must Orphan Boy do to get the Elk Dogs? Why is this difficult?**

_____

_____

_____

219

As Orphan Boy said goodbye, he knelt down at the old man's feet to thank him. As he did, he gently moved aside the edge of the robe. Orphan Boy's eyes widened. Instead of human feet, the grandfather had the shiny hooves of an Elk Dog!

"Ahhh! You know my secret!" the grandfather exclaimed. "Now you can ask for a gift."

The ride home was easy, and Orphan Boy did not arrive empty-handed! When the villagers saw his Elk Dogs, they invited Orphan Boy into their tepees. They gave him gifts and food and called him by his real name at last. Everyone agreed that Long Arrow was the greatest hunter of all!

**Stop** | **Think** | **Write**

**What do the grandfather's feet tell you about him?**

_____

_____

_____

# Look Back and Respond

**1** Why do the people in the village call the animals in the south Elk Dogs? What is our name for this animal?

**Hint**

See pages 215 and 219.

_____

_____

_____

**2** How do the people's opinions of Orphan Boy change during the story? Why does this change occur?

**Hint**

See pages 214 and 220.

_____

_____

_____

**3** What overall message does this story teach?

**Hint**

Almost every page will help you figure out the theme of the story.

_____

_____

_____

**4** What is Orphan Boy's real name?

**Hint**

For a clue, see page 220.

_____

_____

_____

# Be a Reading Detective!

Return to

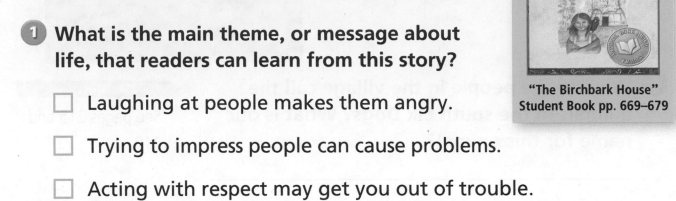

**1** **What is the main theme, or message about life, that readers can learn from this story?**

☐ Laughing at people makes them angry.

☐ Trying to impress people can cause problems.

☐ Acting with respect may get you out of trouble.

**Prove It!** What evidence in the story supports your answer? Check the boxes. ☑ Make notes.

| Evidence | Notes |
|---|---|
| ☐ Omakayas doesn't use the scissors. | |
| ☐ Omakayas stays still. | |
| ☐ Omakayas asks for forgiveness. | |

**Write About It!**

THEME

Answer question **1** using evidence from the text.

_____

_____

_____

_____

_____

_____

_____

**221A**

**2** Which two things happen because Omakayas tries to make friends with the cubs?

☐ The cubs eat berries that Omakayas gives them.

☐ The mother bear comes after Omakayas.

☐ Omakayas brings the cubs home with her.

**Prove It!** What evidence in the story supports your answer? Check the boxes. ☑ Make notes.

| Evidence | Notes |
|---|---|
| ☐ Omakayas holds out her hand. | |
| ☐ Omakayas is flipped on her back. | |
| ☐ Omakayas is pinned down. | |

**Write About It!**

CAUSE AND EFFECT

Answer question **2** using evidence from the text.

_____

_____

_____

_____

_____

_____

# Texas Ranches

**extending
hostile
prospered
residents
sprawling**

Ranching first started in what is now Texas. Mexican cowboys manned the ranches. Then, in 1836, Texas became part of the United States. Some Texans were **hostile** toward Mexicans. They drove many Mexican **residents** out of Texas and claimed the cattle left behind.

In 1861, the Civil War started. Texans went off to fight. The cattle roamed free across the **sprawling** plains. There were huge herds. On returning home, the Texans started rounding them up.

By 1885, just 35 men owned an area **extending** across 30,000 square miles. They owned more than a million cattle. These ranch owners **prospered**!

**1** An area _____ across 30,000 square miles was owned by just 35 men.

**2** When Texas became a state, some Texans were _____ toward Mexicans.

**3** The owners of Texas ranches in the 1880s really _____.

**4** What do the <u>residents</u> of your neighborhood have in common?

_____

_____

_____

**5** People say that Houston is a <u>sprawling</u> city. What do they mean?

_____

_____

_____

# The Cattle Drive

## by Richard Stull

By 1866, most of the beef that was eaten in the East came from Texas. Ranchers in Texas first had to move their cattle to Chicago. That's where the meatpacking plants were. The beef was then packed and shipped by train to eastern cities.

Moving a herd of cattle was called cattle driving. Ranchers hired cowboys to move the cows. About ten or twelve cowboys could move a herd of 3,000 cows.

**Stop** **Think** **Write**

TEXT AND GRAPHIC FEATURES

How does the drawing help you to understand the dangerous conditions of cowboy work?

_____

_____

_____

The cattle drives started in Texas. They ended in Sedalia, Missouri, where there was a railroad. From there, the cows were shipped by train to Chicago.

There was one problem. The trail to Missouri went through farms in eastern Kansas. The **residents** along the trail did not want the cows crossing their land. They thought the cattle carried disease. The cows also trampled and ate the farmers' crops.

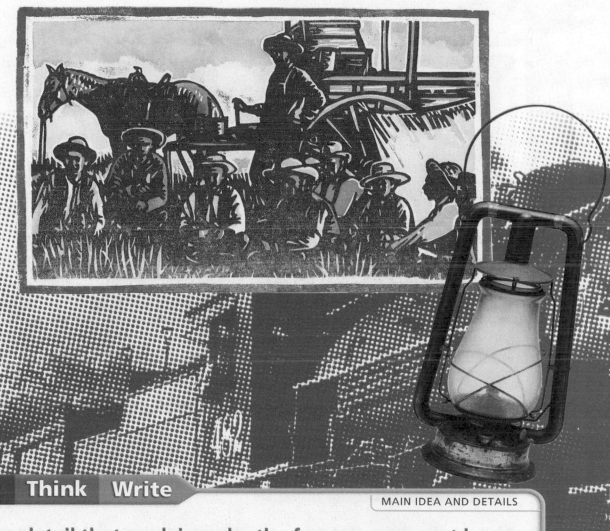

## Stop | Think | Write

MAIN IDEA AND DETAILS

**Give one detail that explains why the farmers were not happy about the cows crossing their land.**

_____

_____

_____

Fights broke out between farmers and cowboys. The cowboys did not want to fight the farmers, so they started moving the cows along a different trail.

This new trail did not go through the farms of eastern Kansas. It ended in a town in western Kansas. The town was Abilene. Abilene also had a railroad **extending** all the way to Chicago.

**Stop** **Think** **Write**

VOCABULARY

Abilene had a railroad <u>extending</u> to Chicago. What does this mean?

_____

_____

_____

A cattle drive was hard work. The trail from Texas to Abilene was about a thousand miles long. The trip could take almost two months. During that time, the cowboys herded the cattle across rivers and small mountain ranges.

During the day, the cowboys drove the herd along the trail. At night, they watched the cattle to guard against thieves and watch for stampedes. The cowboys took turns sleeping and watching.

**Stop** **Think** **Write**

TEXT AND GRAPHIC FEATURES

**What does the drawing tell you about the hardships of cowboy life?**

_____

_____

_____

The cowboys drove the cows over the **sprawling** Indian Territory. The land is now part of Oklahoma. The American Indians there were not **hostile**. In fact, they made money from cattle drives. The cowboys had to pay the tribes ten cents for each cow that passed through their land.

When they reached the railroad in Abilene, the cowboys sold the herd. They then rode back to Texas.

## Stop | Think | Write

VOCABULARY

**What does the author mean by saying that the American Indians were not <u>hostile</u>?**

_____

_____

_____

The time of the great cattle drives lasted about twenty years. In that time, many people **prospered**. Ranchers became rich. Railroads made money. The meatpackers made money. Owners of stores in towns such as Abilene made money. Even the cowboys made money.

**Stop** **Think** **Write**

MAIN IDEA AND DETAILS

**What is the main idea in this paragraph?**

_____

_____

_____

By 1890, things had changed. Railroads ran to Texas and other states in the West. Meatpacking plants had been built throughout the West. The ranchers in Texas did not have to drive their cows to Kansas. The cows did not have to be shipped by train to Chicago. The age of the great cattle drives had come to an end.

**Stop** | **Think** | **Write**

CAUSE AND EFFECT

**What is one reason the great cattle drives ended?**

_____

_____

_____

# Look Back and Respond

**1** **Why did the ranchers in Texas have to move their cows to Chicago?**

_____

_____

_____

**Hint**

For clues, see page 224.

**2** **What details in the story let you know that a cattle drive was hard work?**

_____

_____

_____

**Hint**

You can find clues on pages 226 and 227.

**3** **What graphic source would help to make the cross-country cattle trails more clear for the reader? Explain.**

_____

_____

_____

**Hint**

Think about a graphic source you use when traveling.

**4** **Would you have wanted to go on a cattle drive? Explain.**

_____

_____

_____

**Hint**

Your answers to questions 2 and 3 might help you.

# Be a Reading Detective!

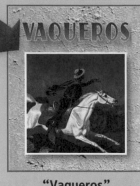

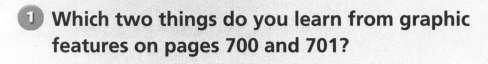

**1** **Which two things do you learn from graphic features on pages 700 and 701?**

☐ where the legendary cities are located

☐ the shape of New Spain

☐ what a longhorn steer looks like

"Vaqueros"
Student Book pp. 697–707

**Prove It!** What evidence in the selection supports your answer? Check the boxes. ☑  Make notes.

| Evidence | Notes |
|---|---|
| ☐ the map on page 700 | |
| ☐ the photo on page 701 | |
| ☐ the caption on page 701 | |

**Write About It!**

TEXT AND GRAPHIC FEATURES

Answer question **1** using evidence from the text.

_____

_____

_____

_____

_____

_____

_____

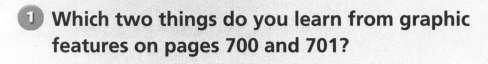

**2** **Which two events led to the start of the vaqueros?**

☐ the introduction of cattle and horses

☐ the invention of barbed wire

☐ Spanish expeditions to the Americas

**Prove It!** What evidence in the selection supports your answer? Check the boxes. ☑ Make notes.

| Evidence | Notes |
|---|---|
| ☐ details about Coronado's trip north | |
| ☐ details about help needed in New Spain | |
| ☐ details about herds spreading out | |

**Write About It!**

SEQUENCE OF EVENTS

**Answer question 2 using evidence from the text.**

_____

_____

_____

_____

_____

_____

_____

✔ TARGET VOCABULARY

beacon
fared
mishap
surged
torment

# The Oregon Trail

Before 1841, it was very difficult to get to the West. People would travel by ship around the tip of South America to reach Oregon! Then the Oregon Trail was discovered. Between 1841 and 1869, hundreds of thousands of people **1** _____ across America along the trail.

The trail followed river valleys. Landmarks along the way, such as Chimney Rock, were a **2** _____ to the travelers. The landmarks could be seen from miles away.

A new kind of wagon was designed for the trail. It **3** _____ much better than the Conestoga wagons that were used before.

Any **4** _____ could delay the wagon train. A broken wheel, an ox losing a shoe, a stampede—all of these would slow down the train.

Another **5** _____ to travelers was the weather. It was either too hot, too wet, or too cold! Most of the journey was done on foot, as the wagons were used to carry possessions.

# Off to Oregon

## by Sheila Boyle

"Maybe you're wondering what's been going on in the store?" Papa asked as we began eating dinner.

"Do you mean all the cleaning and packing?" I asked.

"I've sold the store," Papa said. "Everything here feels too cramped. We're joining a group of families and moving west."

"Leave the city?" The question stuck in my throat.

"Anneke, my dear," Papa whispered. "The government is offering free land out West. If we don't move now, we may never have another chance."

**Stop | Think | Write**

CAUSE AND EFFECT

**Why did Anneke's father want to move to the West?**

_____

_____

_____

A week later my room was empty, and all my favorite things had been sold to strangers. Only essentials could go in the wagon. Everything else had to be left behind.

As we passed the store on our way out of the city, Papa showed no regrets. He remained cheerful even when we had to get rid of more of our possessions. Mama's cooking stove was left by the side of the road. Beside it were my inks and paints. I had one quill left, tucked into the lining of my dress.

**Stop** **Think** **Write**

CAUSE AND EFFECT

**Why do you think they had to get rid of more of their possessions?**

_____

_____

_____

Finally, after six long, hard weeks of traveling, we reached Independence, Missouri. People filled the street, clustering around supply stores and trading posts.

I watched as an Indian girl about my age came out of a shop. Her eyes met mine, and she smiled. I sat down beside her. "Hi," I said, smiling. "Anneke," I said, tapping my chest.

"Geyohi," she said. "Me." She slipped a string of tiny blue beads off her wrist and slid it onto mine. I untied a yellow ribbon from my pigtail and tied it in her hair. I had to leave to help restock our wagon, and when I returned, she had vanished.

**Stop** **Think** **Write**

CAUSE AND EFFECT

**Why did Anneke give Geyohi her yellow ribbon?**

_____

_____

_____

I thought I had made a new friend, but then suddenly she was gone. Now, all I had to look forward to was the rest of our journey. We had 2,000 miles to go. It would take five months.

Almost from the start, we **fared** badly. My little sister, Petra, had a terrible **mishap** as the wagon train tried to cross a river. Water **surged** through the rapids. The ferrymen put the wagons, one by one, on a raft. The oxen swam across. When it was our turn, I heard a scream. Petra had fallen into the water!

"Petra! Head for Rorie!" I yelled, pointing to my favorite ox. Swimming against the current, Petra reached the ox and held tight until he reached the other side.

## Stop　Think　Write

VOCABULARY

**What mishap did Petra have?**

_____

_____

_____

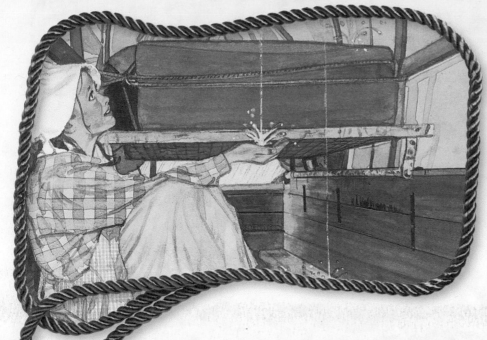

The next few weeks passed in a blur. We endured the **torment** of pelting rain. No matter how we tried to keep the wagons waterproof, the rain found its way in.

Then the land changed. There were no trees, only massive rocks and the dry, scorching prairie. Sometimes at night people talked about what they would build on their new land. I asked, "Does no one live there now?"

"Indians lived there," said the wagon train boss, "but they're gone now." The government had promised the land to the Indians forever. Now the government was breaking its promise.

I walked away, angry. What about Geyohi? Her family needed land, too.

**Stop** **Think** **Write**

VOCABULARY

Why was pelting rain a <u>torment</u> to the members of the wagon train?

_____

_____

_____

One day, we crossed the top of a hill. Fort Hall shone in the early morning sunlight like a **beacon**. We had reached Oregon!

Soon the landscape was lush, green, and full of trees. People cheered. Men threw their hats. Some of them kissed the ground.

My family spent two hard months clearing trees off pasture land. Winter came, and we were still living in our small tarpaper hut. The best news is Papa. He is happy and has great plans for the future. Here he'll build the barn. There, the farmhouse. Over there, the stables.

For my birthday, he had a special surprise for me: a bottle of ink, so I can write in my journal.

## Stop | Think | Write

UNDERSTANDING CHARACTERS

**Describe the relationship between Anneke and her father.**

_____

_____

_____

### How Far in a Day?

On many days, the wagon train would only cover ten to fifteen miles. On rainy or muddy days, it might travel only a single mile. It would take these pioneers five to seven days to travel the distance we can drive by car in a single hour.

### Life and Death on the Oregon Trail

Nearly one in ten people who set off on the Oregon Trail did not survive. The two biggest causes of death were disease and accidents.

### Hard Weather

Fierce thunderstorms, huge hailstones, high winds, snowstorms, lightning, tornadoes, and desert heat persuaded many travelers to turn back.

**Stop Think Write**

CONCLUSIONS AND GENERALIZATIONS

How do these facts help you better understand the courage and resourcefulness of the early pioneers?

_____

_____

_____

# Look Back and Respond

**1** What caused people to undertake such a hard journey across the country in covered wagons?

**Hint**

For clues, see page 234.

_____

_____

_____

**2** How did Anneke help save Petra's life?

**Hint**

For a clue, see page 237.

_____

_____

_____

**3** How would you describe Anneke's father?

**Hint**

For clues, see pages 234 and 239.

_____

_____

_____

**4** What effect do you think traveling west will have on Anneke? Explain your answer.

**Hint**

Clues you can use are on almost every page.

_____

_____

_____

# Be a Reading Detective!

Return to

"Rachel's Journal"
Student Book pp. 725–735

**1** **Why did the adults forbid Rachel and the children from ever walking along the cut-offs?**

☐ They were worried that the children would get lost again.

☐ They were concerned about extremely bad weather.

☐ They feared the children might run into hostile Indians.

**Prove It!** What evidence in the story supports your answer?
Check the boxes. ☑ Make notes.

| Evidence | Notes |
|---|---|
| ☐ events on the cut-offs | |
| ☐ events when the children get back | |
| ☐ | |

**Write About It!**

CAUSE AND EFFECT

Answer question **1** using evidence from the text.

_____

_____

_____

_____

_____

_____

_____

**2** Why were the women on the wagons "first joyous and then mad" when Rachel and the children returned?

☐ They were happy to see the children, but angry about the state of the clothing.

☐ They were glad the children were safe, but angry because they had been worried.

☐ other _____

**Prove It!** What evidence in the story supports your answer? Check the boxes. ☑ Make notes.

| Evidence | Notes |
|---|---|
| ☐ events of May 16 | |
| ☐ adults' worries about what might happen | |
| ☐ | |

**Write About It!**

CONCLUSIONS AND GENERALIZATIONS

Answer question **2** using evidence from the text.

_____
_____
_____
_____
_____
_____
_____

# Early American Explorers

In the early 1800s, explorers traveled long distances on foot. Back then, a **trek** could go on for hundreds of miles. The explorers walked and walked.

An **expedition** could last for months or even years. The goal might be to explore a new area or to find better routes between places.

Crossing a mountain **range** was a challenge. The explorers could not walk around a group of mountains. Often they relied on local people to show them the best ways across the mountains.

Many trips stopped during the winter. It was difficult to travel in the snow. The trips **resumed** in spring, when the weather improved.

Often the explorers **fulfilled** their goals and found what they expected. Even if they didn't, their efforts weren't wasted. Every new piece of information about the land was useful.

1. After stopping for the winter, trips _____ in spring.

2. Explorers might be on an _____ for months or even years.

3. It was a challenge for the explorers to cross a mountain _____.

4. Would you prefer to take a <u>trek</u> in a rainforest or on a snowy mountain? Explain.

_____

_____

_____

5. Tell about a goal or dream that you have already <u>fulfilled</u>.

_____

_____

_____

# Protector of the Wilderness

## by Mia Lewis

Even as a small boy, John Muir loved being out in nature. He worked hard on his father's farm. He had very little free time, but he spent as much of it as he could exploring the natural world.

John Muir didn't have much formal education. Most of what he knew he taught himself. He woke up very early every day to read on his own before work began. Muir was also an inventor. One of his inventions was an alarm clock that tipped him out of bed!

### Stop | Think | Write

MAIN IDEA AND DETAILS

Muir read every day before his work began. What main idea does this detail support?

_____

_____

_____

Later, Muir went to a university for a few years. Soon he left it, saying he preferred the "University of the Wilderness." He hiked to Canada, where he worked in a broom factory. He returned to the United States after the factory burned down.

Muir was working in Indiana when he injured his eye. For one scary month, he could not see, but his injury changed his life. He decided to travel and spend as much time outside as possible. He set out on a 1,000-mile trek to the Gulf of Mexico.

**Stop** **Think** **Write**

AUTHOR'S PURPOSE

**Why does the author put the phrase "University of the Wilderness" inside quotation marks?**

_____

_____

_____

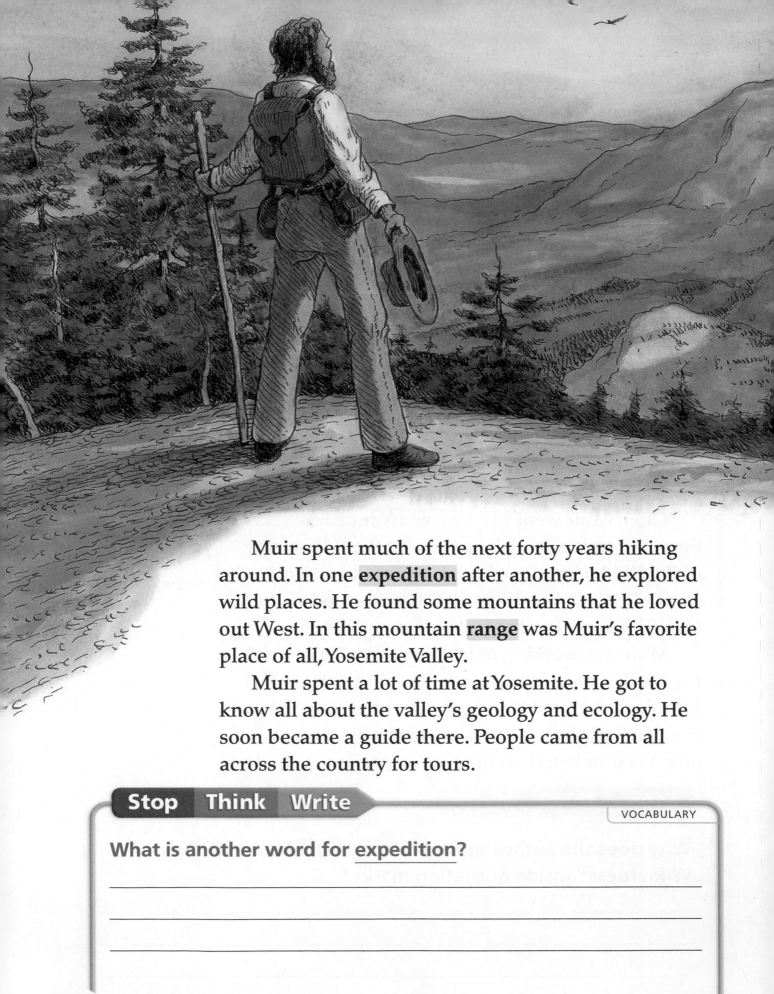

Muir spent much of the next forty years hiking around. In one **expedition** after another, he explored wild places. He found some mountains that he loved out West. In this mountain **range** was Muir's favorite place of all, Yosemite Valley.

Muir spent a lot of time at Yosemite. He got to know all about the valley's geology and ecology. He soon became a guide there. People came from all across the country for tours.

**Stop** | **Think** | **Write**

VOCABULARY

**What is another word for expedition?**

_____

_____

_____

Muir was more than just a tour guide for Yosemite. He also worked to protect the area. He wanted it to stay wild. He was happy when Congress created Yosemite National Park. No one would be allowed to develop the land.

Yosemite wasn't Muir's only concern. He founded the Sierra Club to save all wild places. The club worked to protect natural areas. It is still going strong!

**Stop** **Think** **Write**

CONCLUSIONS

**What does it mean when the author says that the Sierra Club is still going strong?**

_____

_____

_____

After he married, Muir moved to a farm and had two children. He was not happy staying in one place. He soon **resumed** his travels and his writing.

In all, Muir wrote ten books and three hundred magazine articles. The articles came out in all the major magazines of the day. This meant that his words reached a large group of people. They paid attention to what he had to say.

**Stop** | **Think** | **Write**

When Muir <u>resumed</u> his travels, did he stay on his farm? Explain.

_____

_____

_____

Some people value land for the ways they can make money from it. Muir said that untouched land was valuable. He thought that unspoiled wilderness is the greatest treasure of all.

Muir's ideas changed the way people thought. They even changed how the President of the United States thought. President Theodore Roosevelt spent three days camping with Muir. He listened to Muir's ideas, and later he set aside land for national parks, forests, and monuments.

**Stop** **Think** **Write**

MAIN IDEA AND DETAILS

**How did Muir's ideas affect the way the United States is now?**

_____

_____

_____

John Muir changed our country. He worked to save Yosemite and many other wild areas. The goals he fought for were **fulfilled** when Congress created the National Park Service. That was just two years after Muir died. Today, everyone can visit the National Parks.

Muir fought his whole life to protect the environment. What if John Muir were alive today? He would be a very busy man!

**Stop** **Think** **Write**

INFER/PREDICT

What does the author mean when she says John Muir would be a busy man if he were alive today?

_____

_____

_____

# Look Back and Respond

**1** How did an accident change John Muir's life forever?

_____

_____

_____

**Hint**
For a clue, see pages 245.

**2** What was the author's purpose for writing about John Muir?

_____

_____

_____

**Hint**
Clues are on every page!

**3** What details support the idea that Muir had a major impact on the country and its people?

_____

_____

_____

**Hint**
Clues are on every page!

**4** What are some things that Muir started or worked for in his lifetime that are still around today?

_____

_____

_____

**Hint**
For clues, see pages 247, 249, and 250.

# Be a Reading Detective!

Return to

Cornerstones of Freedom
Lewis and Clark

R. Conrad Stein

"Lewis and Clark"
Student Book pp. 753–763

**1** How does the author support the main idea of how difficult it would be to cross the Rockies?

☐ with details about the environment, Sacagawea, and weather

☐ with details about the weather, environment, and food

☐ with details about food, pack animals, and Sacagawea

**Prove It!** What evidence in the selection supports your answer? Check the boxes. ☑ Make notes.

| Evidence | Notes |
|---|---|
| ☐ description of the trails | |
| ☐ details about the weather | |
| ☐ details about the lack of game | |

## Write About It!

MAIN IDEAS AND DETAILS

Answer question **1** using evidence from the text.

_____

_____

_____

_____

_____

_____

_____

**2** **What happened as a result of the meeting with Chief Cameahwait? Choose all correct answers.**

☐ The chief gave them a guide.

☐ The chief gave them horses.

☐ Sacagawea was reunited with her brother.

**Prove It!** What evidence in the selection supports your answer? Check the boxes. ☑ Make notes.

| Evidence | Notes |
|---|---|
| ☐ Sacagawea's behavior at the meeting | |
| ☐ how the Shoshone acted at the meeting | |
| ☐ details about what the chief gave them | |

St. Louis

**Write About It!**

CAUSE AND EFFECT

**Answer question 2 using evidence from the text.**

_____

_____

_____

_____

_____

_____

_____

# Animal Migration

✓ TARGET VOCABULARY

disturbing
gorgeous
gradually
identical
struggled

Many animals migrate each year. They travel from one place to another. They return later in the year to the **1** _____ spot they left from! This is amazing, as some of the animals have traveled huge distances.

A colorful flock of hundreds or thousands of migrating birds can be a **2** _____ sight. The Manx Shearwater is a bird that can live for 50 years. Each year, it migrates from Europe to South America and back. This bird travels at least a million miles in its life!

Flying such distances is hard. Swimming is even harder! Some gray whales migrate from Alaska to Mexico and back again. The whales' trip progresses very **3** _____ . They travel only about three miles each hour.

Penguins and fish also migrate by swimming. Pacific salmon migrate between salt water and fresh water. They travel hundreds of miles from the ocean upstream in rivers. When people built dams, the salmon **4** _____ to complete their journey. So, people built fish ladders at the dams. Now the salmon do not find the migration so **5** _____ .

# The Long Flight

by Mia Lewis

## The Monarch's Migration

It is late August on the border of Canada and the United States. A **gorgeous** monarch butterfly has just **struggled** out of its chrysalis. This butterfly is different from its parents and grandparents. It will not lay eggs right away like most females. It will live much longer than the monarchs that were born earlier in the summer.

This butterfly will make an amazing journey. So will millions just like it. They will make their way to winter homes in Mexico and southern California.

**Stop** **Think** **Write**

VOCABULARY

Based on the illustrations, do you agree that the monarch butterfly is <u>gorgeous</u>? Why?

_____

_____

_____

The monarch will fly high. It may fly almost two miles up in the sky. Its wings will beat from five to twelve times every second. It will fly thousands of miles to a place it has never seen.

Soon millions of monarchs will be in the air. A monarch usually lives alone. Now it travels with a large group of other monarchs. They will sip nectar from flowers along the way. This gives them the energy they need for the long trip.

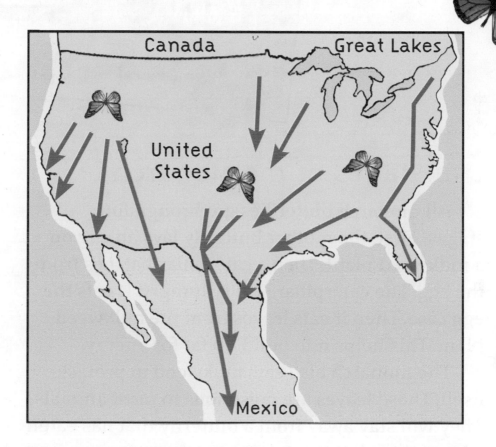

**Stop** **Think** **Write**

TEXT AND GRAPHIC FEATURES

**Look at the map. What is the destination for butterflies that start out near the Great Lakes?**

_____

_____

_____

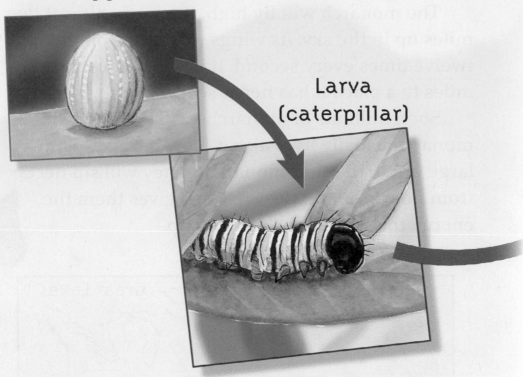

Egg

Larva
(caterpillar)

## Life Stages of the Monarch

All monarch butterflies go through four
stages. First, the mother butterfly lays an egg on
a milkweed plant. Then a caterpillar hatches from
the egg. The caterpillar is very hungry. It eats the
egg case. Then it eats leaves from the milkweed
plant. This helps it to build up fat for energy.

The monarch also eats milkweed to protect
itself. These leaves are poisonous to most animals.
They will stay away from a butterfly that has eaten
a lot of this plant!

**Stop  Think  Write**

TEXT AND GRAPHIC FEATURES

**Look at the diagram on this page. What are two names for the
second stage in the monarch's life?**

_____

_____

_____

Chrysalis

Adult
(butterfly)

The caterpillar makes a chrysalis. Inside, it **gradually** changes. Finally, a butterfly crawls out! It rests. It waits for its wings to dry. When they are dry, the monarch will be able to fly. All monarchs are orange and black. They all look very similar. But they are not **identical**.

Shorter days and cooler weather tell the monarch it is time to leave. It sets off on its long flight. Scientists do not know how it can tell where to go. They think it might use the position of the sun to help it figure out which direction to go.

**Stop** | **Think** | **Write**

SEQUENCE OF EVENTS

**Write the stages of a monarch's life in order: chrysalis, egg, butterfly, larva.**

_____

_____

_____

**257**

## Flying South

The distance to the monarch's winter grounds can be as long as three thousand miles. Wind or weather can take the butterfly out of its way, too. The monarch stops flying if the wind is too strong. It stops if it is raining or too hot.

The journey takes about two months. When the monarch finally arrives, there will be millions of other butterflies there. Each year the monarchs return to the same exact trees. They huddle together on the branches to keep warm.

**Stop** **Think** **Write**

CAUSE AND EFFECT

**Why would a monarch stop flying if the wind is strong?**

_____

_____

_____

# Flying Back Home

Thousands and thousands of monarchs crowd together through the winter. Spring finally arrives. The monarch gets ready for the journey home. It will not make it all the way back, though. It will die along the way.

The monarch lays eggs before it dies. These eggs will hatch. The offspring will go through all the same stages and become butterflies. Then they will continue the long trip back to their summer home.

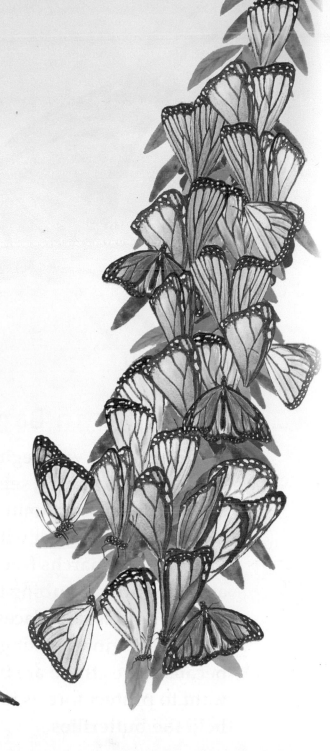

## Stop | Think | Write

TEXT AND GRAPHIC FEATURES

**What does the picture on this page show?**

_____

_____

_____

## Monarchs in Danger

The pattern will begin again. Summer will come and go. Several sets of monarchs will live their lives. Then autumn will draw near. The last monarchs of summer will get ready for their trip.

Today, monarchs face new dangers. Human activities are **disturbing** their way of life. There aren't enough safe places left for them anymore. Even their winter resting spots are in danger because trees there are being cut down. Scientists want to protect forests in these areas. That will help the butterflies.

**Stop** | **Think** | **Write**

VOCABULARY

**What is one way that humans are disturbing the monarchs' way of life?**

_____

_____

_____

# Look Back and Respond

**1** What is special about the last monarch butterflies to be born each summer?

_____

_____

_____

**Hint**

For clues, see page 254.

**2** How high can a monarch butterfly fly?

_____

_____

_____

**Hint**

For a clue, see page 255.

**3** What does the map on page 255 tell you about where in the United States you can find monarch butterflies in the summer?

_____

_____

_____

**Hint**

In what parts of the country do the arrows begin?

**4** What is so amazing about the monarch's journey to its winter resting place?

_____

_____

_____

**Hint**

For clues, see pages 255 and 258.

# Be a Reading Detective!

"Animals on the Move"
Student Magazine pp. 6–13

**1** Why are the captions and photos on pages 9 and 11 helpful?

☐ They make the magazine more fun to read.

☐ They tell things not found in the text.

☐ They show a honeycomb.

**Prove It!** What evidence in the selection supports your answer? Check the boxes. ☑ Make notes.

| Evidence | Notes |
|---|---|
| ☐ details of waggling and circle dancing | |
| ☐ information about how some cranes learn to migrate | |
| ☐ | |

## Write About It!

TEXT AND GRAPHIC FEATURES

Answer question **1** using evidence from the text.

_____

_____

_____

_____

_____

_____

_____

261A

**2** **What is the main idea of the section "Returning Home"?**

☐ Salmon swim upriver.

☐ Salmon use the earth's magnetic field.

☐ Salmon return to the place of their birth.

**Prove It!** What evidence in the selection supports your answer?
Check the boxes. ☑ Make notes.

| Evidence | Notes |
|---|---|
| ☐ details about the salmon life cycle | |
| ☐ details in the caption | |
| ☐ | |

**Write About It!**

MAIN IDEAS AND DETAILS

Answer question **2** using evidence from the text.

_____

_____

_____

_____

_____

_____

_____

**adapted
available
conserving
procedure
resemble**

# A Guide for a Cave

A cave tour guide takes visitors through the cave. He knows everything about the special landscape inside the cave. He knows which areas are **①** _____ to visit and which areas are too dangerous or far away to explore.

The guide uses special equipment that is **②** _____ for use in a cave. For example, his hardhat is not a regular hardhat. It is equipped with a bright light. This lights up the cave in front of him.

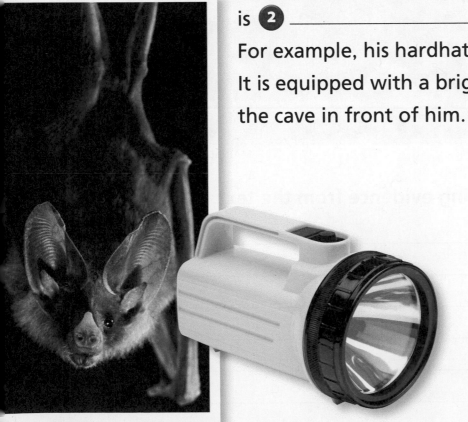

A visitor to the cave might get lost without a guide. Many of the paths and chambers in the cave ③ _____ each other. The visitor might not be able to tell them apart. Luckily, the guide knows each one.

Part of the job is ④ _____ the cave. The guide has to protect it from damage. He has to make sure that the visitors do not leave trash behind them.

Too many people visiting the cave at once would be a problem. One ⑤ _____ that is followed to protect the cave is to limit the number of people on the tour each day.

# A Trip to a Cave

## by Mia Lewis

"Welcome to the world of caves!" said Professor Collins. The group of explorers was standing at the mouth of a dark cave. "This is Min. She is a videographer from a nature website. She'll be filming our trip today."

"I think your website's cave exhibit is cool," said Hadley. He was one of the explorers.

"Hey, thanks, but I didn't make that exhibit. This is actually my first trip into a cave!" Min said.

"Well, don't worry," said Hadley. "You'll be fine."

## Stop | Think | Write

UNDERSTANDING CHARACTERS

**What is your first impression of Hadley? Explain.**

_____

_____

_____

"Cave explorers are called spelunkers," said Jordan. "The study of caves is called speleology."

"The terrain in these caves can be dangerous," said Professor Collins. "Some areas are not **available** for visitors to explore. We must be sure to follow the **procedure** for cave visitors."

"Which way do we go?" asked Lane. "All of the paths **resemble** each other." He looked nervous.

"Yes, that's why it's easy to get lost," warned the professor. "I know these caves, though. Let's just make sure we all stick together."

Professor Collins took the lead. The group started down the dark tunnel.

## Stop Think Write

VOCABULARY

If two paths <u>resemble</u> each other, do they look similar or very different?

_____

_____

_____

265

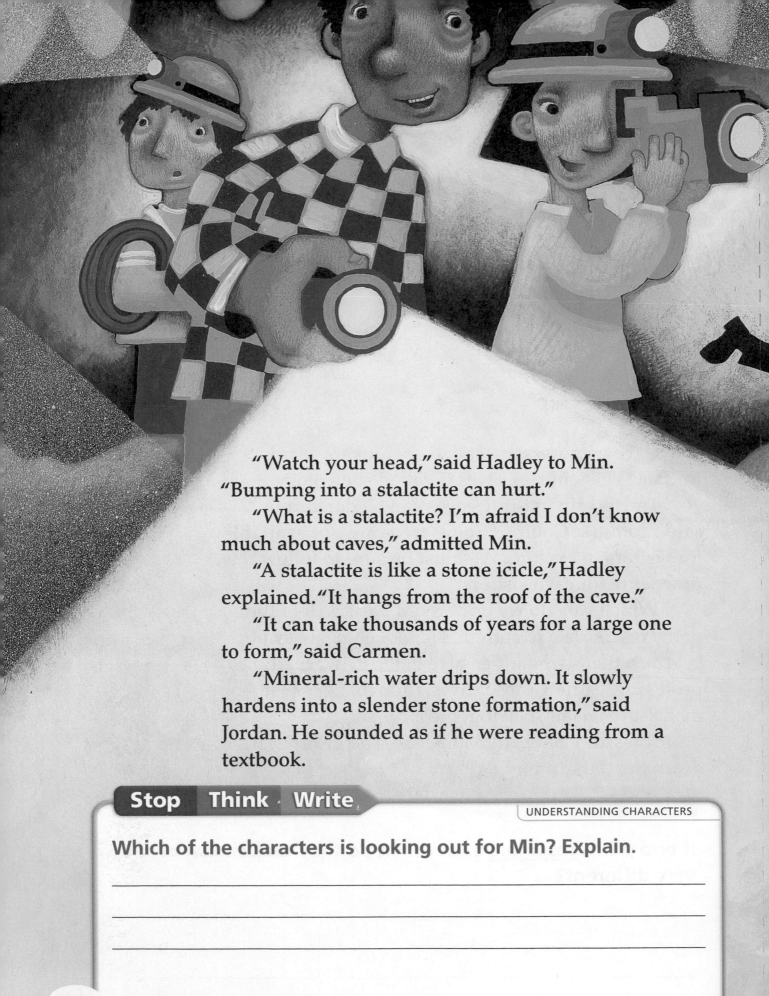

"Watch your head," said Hadley to Min. "Bumping into a stalactite can hurt."

"What is a stalactite? I'm afraid I don't know much about caves," admitted Min.

"A stalactite is like a stone icicle," Hadley explained. "It hangs from the roof of the cave."

"It can take thousands of years for a large one to form," said Carmen.

"Mineral-rich water drips down. It slowly hardens into a slender stone formation," said Jordan. He sounded as if he were reading from a textbook.

## Stop | Think | Write

**Which of the characters is looking out for Min? Explain.**

_____

_____

_____

"Stalactites can be colored by different minerals," added the professor. "They can be red, blue, yellow, or other colors."

"Are these also stalactites on the cave floor?" asked Min.

"No! Those are stalagmites," explained Carmen. "They form from falling water droplets. I love them!"

Professor Collins told them that the rock forms weren't as strong as they looked. He warned them not to touch anything. **Conserving** the treasures of the cave was just as important as exploring it. Min got a good shot of the scene.

## Stop | Think | Write

CAUSE AND EFFECT

**Why do stalagmites rise up from the cave floor?**

_____

_____

_____

"Our website shows films of animals, too," said Min. "Do you think we'll see any?"

"Maybe," said Hadley. "We'll have to look closely. Most animals in caves are very small. There are a few larger ones as well."

"Many of the animals in caves are like the ones outside," said Carmen. "Still, there's one big difference. They're blind."

"They have **adapted** to the total darkness of the cave," said Jordan. "Sight wouldn't help them here. They use their other senses to get around."

**Stop** **Think** **Write**

VOCABULARY

Why have animals in caves <u>adapted</u> to live without eyesight?

_____

_____

_____

"Look! A crayfish!" said Carmen. "Cool!"

"Bats also live in caves," said Jordan. "They aren't blind, though, whatever people say."

"Aren't bats dangerous?" asked Lane. "Don't they carry diseases?"

"Well, some bats do carry rabies. It's best to avoid contact with them," warned Hadley. "Don't worry. Bats will want to avoid you, too!"

"Bats are helpful in checking the number of insects. They eat thousands every night," explained Jordan. "One small bat can eat about 600 insects an hour!"

**Stop** **Think** **Write**

UNDERSTANDING CHARACTERS

**How would you describe Lane?**

_____

_____

_____

"Guys! Shine your flashlights up!" said Carmen.

"What are those furry things up there?" gasped Lane.

"Hmm. I think those are gray bats," replied Jordan.

"Wow!" said Min. "Look how many there are! I hope we didn't disturb them. Do they usually move around so much?"

"Only when they are getting ready for a flight!" said Hadley.

"Quick!" said Carmen. "Everybody, duck! Make way for the bats!"

**Stop** | **Think** | **Write**

INFER AND PREDICT

**Do you think the explorers are in danger? Explain your answer.**

_____

_____

_____

# Look Back and Respond

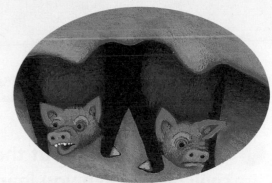

**1** **What do spelunkers do?**

_____

_____

_____

**Hint**

For a clue, see page 265.

**2** **How much does Min know about caves? Explain.**

_____

_____

_____

**Hint**

For clues, see pages 266 and 267.

**3** **Write three words to describe Jordan.**

_____

_____

_____

**Hint**

Look for clues throughout the story.

**4** **Compare Carmen and Lane. Which one is having more fun?**

_____

_____

_____

**Hint**

Look for clues throughout the story.

# Be a Reading Detective!

Return to

**"Mysteries at Cliff Palace"**
**Student Magazine pp. 20–27**

**1** **What message about the mysteries of past civilizations can you learn from this play?**

☐ It is impossible to know anything about the past.

☐ Some mysteries may never be solved.

☐ Mesa Verde is an amazing place.

**Prove It!** What evidence in the play supports your answer?
Check the boxes. ✔ Make notes.

| Evidence | Notes |
|---|---|
| ☐ what Ruben tries to figure out | |
| ☐ what the ranger says | |
| ☐ the photos | |

## Write About It!

THEME

Answer question **1** using evidence from the text.

_____

_____

_____

_____

_____

_____

**2** **Which words describe Ruben?** Choose every correct answer.

☐ curious          ☐ absent-minded

☐ determined      ☐ lazy

**Prove It!** What evidence in the play supports your answer?
Check the boxes. ☑ Make notes.

| Evidence | Notes |
|---|---|
| ☐ details about Ruben's losing things | |
| ☐ details about Ruben's curiosity | |
| ☐ details about Ruben's ideas | |

**Write About It!**

UNDERSTANDING CHARACTERS

Answer question **2** using evidence from the text.

_____

_____

_____

_____

_____

_____

_____

aspects
previously
rural
surveyed
viewpoint

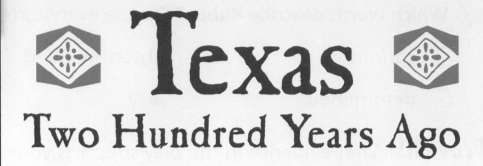

# Texas
## Two Hundred Years Ago

Texas is different now than it was long ago. One of the **❶** _____ of Texas that has changed is ownership of the land. Originally, the land was occupied only by American Indians. There were no cities. The area was completely **❷** _____.

▲ **A pueblo**

▲ **A Spanish building in San Antonio**

Texas is now part of the United States. It was  _____ owned, at different times, by Mexico, Spain, and France. The  _____ of these nations was the same: we own Texas. The only thing that changed was the "we."

Two hundred years ago, Texas was a Spanish state. Spanish explorers and mapmakers had 5 _____ Texas for several hundred years. The Spanish built the towns of San Antonio, Goliad, and Nacogdoches. Even so, only about 7,000 people lived in Texas two hundred years ago.

# The Many Faces of Rolling Hills

**by Richard Stull**

Do you know Rolling Hills? It's a small town near High Falls Park, about twenty miles outside the city. I had hardly given the place a thought until last month. That's when Mom and I went there to visit my aunt.

One great thing about our visit was the peach cobbler that my aunt made. Another great thing was what I learned about Rolling Hills. It gave me a whole new **viewpoint** on the area. It also made me think differently about the places where people live.

## Stop | Think | Write

What is the writer's <u>viewpoint</u> on his aunt's peach cobbler?

_____

_____

_____

My aunt moved to Rolling Hills three months ago. Her house looks brand-new. In my mind, the whole town looks brand-new. The streets are lined with houses, so I guess a lot of families live there. I saw kids playing together in the yards and cycling along the streets. It's a great place to live.

**Stop** **Think** **Write**

FACT AND OPINION

**List one opinion and one fact that the writer expresses in the paragraph.**

_____

_____

_____

I was in my aunt's yard when I noticed an old building in the distance. Its walls had fallen down. I asked my aunt what the old building was doing in a new neighborhood like Rolling Hills.

My aunt told me that Rolling Hills had not always been like it is now. She said that all of the land around there had **previously** been a farm. I was amazed. I couldn't believe that all the houses and yards were built on what had once been farmland.

**Stop  Think  Write**

**What does the writer's aunt mean when she says that the land had <u>previously</u> been a farm?**

_____

_____

_____

I asked my aunt about other **aspects** of Rolling Hills that used to be different. Of course, she told me to visit a library to find out. Aunts are always like that. Still, I did as she suggested.

The local librarian helped me find newspaper stories about Rolling Hills. Sure enough, it had once been a big farm with a farmhouse and a barn. Cattle grazed in fields where houses now stand.

**Stop  Think  Write**

FACT AND OPINION

**Does the sentence "Aunts are always like that" state a fact or an opinion? Explain.**

_____

_____

_____

Then I got to thinking about what the whole area had been like before it was a farm. This time the librarian pointed out several books about the history of the county. From my reading, I learned that two hundred years ago, Rolling Hills was not a farm at all. It was all forest. There was no park nearby, and there was no city. The library wasn't here, either.

Settlers came here, **surveyed** the land, and decided that they were the only people around. Of course, they were wrong.

Stop Think Write

INFER AND PREDICT

**Describe the area of Rolling Hills two hundred years ago.**

_____

_____

_____

American Indians lived in the area. They had lived here for hundreds of years before the settlers arrived. Back then, all the land in these parts was a thick forest. The people lived here for centuries without changing the land.

The Indians hunted in the forest and fished in the streams. The summers were probably very pretty. The winters were most likely quite harsh.

**Stop** **Think** **Write**

FACT AND OPINION

**Which sentence in the last paragraph states a fact? Explain.**

_____

_____

_____

I know it's hard to believe that this busy town was once completely **rural**. It's true, though.

So far, I've discovered that Rolling Hills is way more interesting than I would have believed, and I've researched only what the area was like a few hundred years ago. I wonder what it was like a thousand years ago, or ten thousand years ago. There might have been different kinds of trees. The hills might not have been as steep. Maybe musk oxen and mastodons lived here. Perhaps there were even saber-toothed tigers, too!

**Stop** **Think** **Write**

CONCLUSIONS AND GENERALIZATIONS

**What does the writer learn about Rolling Hills that is true for most places?**

_____

_____

_____

# Look Back and Respond

**1** **What is the writer's opinion of studying local history?**

_____

_____

_____

> **Hint**
> You can find clues throughout the story.

**2** **What first got the writer thinking about how places change?**

_____

_____

_____

> **Hint**
> For clues, see page 276.

**3** **How is the area of Rolling Hills today different from the way it was two hundred years ago?**

_____

_____

_____

> **Hint**
> You can find clues throughout the story.

**4** **Why does the writer's aunt suggest that he visit the local library?**

_____

_____

_____

> **Hint**
> For clues, see page 277.

# Be a Reading Detective!

Return to

**"Fossils"**
**Student Magazine pp. 36–41**

**1** **"Mary Anning was the greatest fossilist the world ever knew."** Which facts support this opinion?

☐ Anning discovered the first ichthyosaur fossil.

☐ Jared Post found a woolly mammoth tooth.

☐ Someone said Anning understood fossils more than professors.

**Prove It!** What evidence in the selection supports your answer? Check the boxes. ✓ Make notes.

| Evidence | Notes |
|---|---|
| ☐ facts about Anning's discoveries | |
| ☐ statements by others about Anning | |
| ☐ Anning's handling of fossils | |

## Write About It!

FACT AND OPINION

Answer question **1** using evidence from the text.

_____

_____

_____

_____

_____

_____

_____

**2** **Why does the author tell about young people who found fossils?**

☐ to prove that mammoth teeth can still be found

☐ to make the subject more interesting for young readers

☐ to show that only young people are interested in fossils

**Prove It!** What evidence in the selection supports your answer?
Check the boxes. ☑  Make notes.

| Evidence | Notes |
|---|---|
| ☐ details about the young fossil finders | |
| ☐ photos of Jared and Kaleb | |
| ☐ | |

**Write About It!**

AUTHOR'S PURPOSE

**Answer question ② using evidence from the text.**

_____

_____

_____

_____

_____

_____

# Blown Off Course

No one really knows how birds find their way as they migrate. Whatever method they use, it is very ❶ _____ . A bird may travel thousands of miles and end up at the exact same spot as the year before.

Bird migrations take place at the same time as fall storms and hurricanes. The birds are heading for a particular ❷ _____ , but the wind can blow them off course.

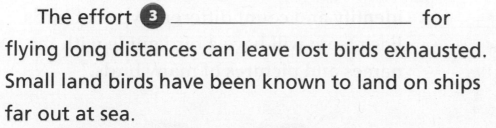

The effort **3** _____ for flying long distances can leave lost birds exhausted. Small land birds have been known to land on ships far out at sea.

In the fall of 2008, bird watchers in Scotland photographed a small American bird, the red-eyed vireo. It had traveled 3,000 miles. That's really an **4** _____ long trip for such a small bird.

Scientists who study birds have had new **5** _____ into bird populations. They think that many of the bird colonies on remote islands are the result of birds being blown off course.

# Counting Birds

### by Mia Lewis

A group of students are at Matagorda Island, part of the Aransas National Wildlife Refuge. They reached their **destination** in the morning. They are there for fun and also to do a job.

"You're going to help us with a bird count," says Ranger Lucia.

"You'll work in three teams: Red, Green, and Blue," says Ranger Mark. "Your job is to identify and count different types of birds. Each team will have a bird guide with the names and pictures of many birds."

## Stop | Think | Write

CAUSE AND EFFECT

**Why are the students at the wildlife refuge?**

_____

_____

_____

"There's a special way to count," says Lucia. "Only record the highest number of birds you see together at one time. Here's how it works. Let's say you see a group of three sparrows. You write that down. Later you see a group of five sparrows. You write that down. Then you see a group of two sparrows. You do not write that down because you have already seen a larger group."

Mark added, "Your record book would say *Sparrows: 3, 5. High count = 5.* Only the 5 goes into the final count. That way you're sure that you haven't counted the same birds more than once."

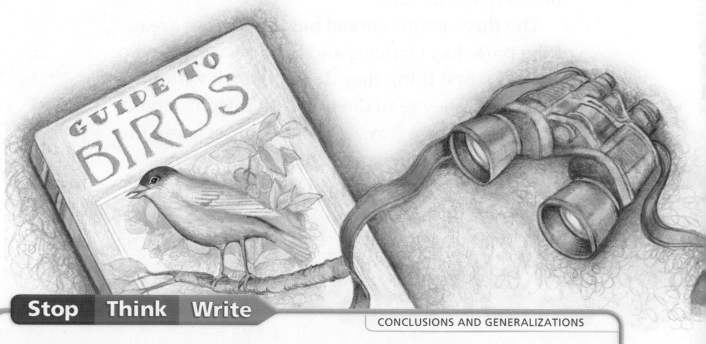

### Stop | Think | Write

CONCLUSIONS AND GENERALIZATIONS

Why wouldn't a team record a group of two sparrows after it had recorded a group of five sparrows?

_____

_____

_____

"Got it?" asks Mark. "Good! Off you go. Meet us back here in one hour."

The three teams spread out to different areas of the park. Joe, Darlene, and Bill are on the Red Team. The first thing they do is sit down with their guidebook. They read the tips with **insights** about the most **effective** ways to identify birds using the way they fly and their size, coloring, and songs.

"I can help identify the birds," says Joe. "My parents are bird watchers."

"Great!" says Darlene. "Let's go."

| Stop | Think | Write |

VOCABULARY

**Why will Joe be an <u>effective</u> member of the Red Team?**

_____

_____

_____

Emma, Josh, and Tia are on the Blue Team. They start out without looking at the guidebook. Pretty soon they see some birds.

"Look!" says Emma. "Little yellow birds!"

"Does anyone know what they are?" asks Tia.

"Not me," says Josh. "That's an **incredibly** bright yellow. Let's see if we can find them in the book."

"Check this picture," says Tia. "I think these are American goldfinches."

"I agree," says Emma. "Quick! Let's count how many we see before they fly away. One, two, three…"

**Stop** **Think** **Write**

COMPARE AND CONTRAST

**In what way is the Blue Team's method different from the Red Team's?**

_____

_____

_____

The Green Team is walking toward the water. Sam, Beth, and Alec stop when they hear a honking noise. They turn to look and see a huge bird standing in the water.

"Wow!" says Alec. "Look at that giant bird! It must be as tall as a person."

"Look in the guidebook," says Sam. "Let's see what it is."

"It's a whooping crane!" says Beth.

"I think you're right," says Sam. "It's mostly white like the bird in the picture. It also has the same black and red patch on its head."

**Stop** **Think** **Write**

SUMMARIZE

**How does the Green Team identify the crane?**

_____

_____

_____

"The guide says that whooping cranes stand nearly five feet tall," says Beth. "They have a wingspan of seven feet."

"They travel in pairs or as a family," says Sam.

"Look at this," says Alec, pointing to the page in the book. "They are an endangered species. They are in trouble."

"That's why refuges like this are **required**. The cranes need them so that they can make a comeback," says Beth. "Hey, guys, let's see if we can find the whole family."

## Stop | Think | Write

VOCABULARY

Why are refuges **required** for some kinds of wildlife?

_____

_____

_____

Very soon, the hour is up. The teams meet back up with the rangers.

"We saw two quails," says Joe for the Red Team.

"The Blue Team saw four American goldfinches," says Emma.

"We saw five whooping cranes," says Alec. "The Green Team wins!"

"Yes," says Ranger Lucia. "All the information the teams gathered is useful. It will help scientists understand how birds adapt to changes in their environment."

"Good job everyone!" says Ranger Mark. "Come back next year and help us count birds again!"

## Stop | Think | Write

CONCLUSIONS AND GENERALIZATIONS

Do you think the field trip was more fun because the students had the job of counting birds? Explain.

_____

_____

_____

# Look Back and Respond

**1** How do the bird guides help the students identify birds?

**Hint**
For clues, see pages 286 through 289.

_____

_____

_____

**2** Why are wildlife refuges important?

**Hint**
For clues, see page 289.

_____

_____

_____

**3** Why do you think the rangers divide the students into three teams?

**Hint**
Think about the job that the students are going to do.

_____

_____

_____

**4** Is the trip to the wildlife refuge a success? Explain.

**Hint**
Look at the first and last pages of the story.

_____

_____

_____

# Be a Reading Detective!

Return to

"The Case of
the Missing Deer"
Student Magazine pp. 52–57

**1** What can you say about deer based on
the story?

☐ Deer do not like apples.

☐ Deer are afraid of people.

☐ Deer travel in groups.

**Prove It!** What evidence in the story supports your answer?
Check the boxes. ☑ Make notes.

| Evidence | Notes |
|---|---|
| ☐ details about the sweatshirt | |
| ☐ what the deer do | |
| ☐ | |

**Write About It!**

CONCLUSIONS AND GENERALIZATIONS

Answer question **1** using evidence from the text.

_____

_____

_____

_____

_____

_____

_____

**2** **Which event happens first?**

☐ Blake removes his sweatshirt from the chair.

☐ The deer eat apples in Blake's yard.

☐ The children play soccer in Blake's yard.

**Prove It!** What evidence in the story supports your answer?
Check the boxes. ☑ Make notes.

| Evidence | Notes |
|---|---|
| ☐ the order of events in the text | |
| ☐ the illustrations | |
| ☐ | |

**Write About It!**

SEQUENCE OF EVENTS

Answer question **2** using evidence from the text.

_____

_____

_____

_____

_____

_____

# Discovering the Past

Our plan was to search for signs of an ancient civilization. At the site, there were mounds of earth **extending** over a large area. The mounds stretched from the river all the way to the bottom of a cliff.

There was **undoubtedly** something under those mounds. We began to dig. We went at a slow **pace**. We didn't want to damage whatever was there.

Before too long, we realized that we had **underestimated** how important our discovery would be. We thought we might find a few old pots and coins. Instead, we discovered the remains of a whole town!

The town was completely covered with layers of dirt. From the items we found, we **reasoned** that the town was thousands of years old! We decided to call more experts for help.

**1** The team dug at a slow _____ so they wouldn't damage anything.

**2** Based on what they found, the team _____ that the town was thousands of years old.

**3** There were mounds of earth _____ over an area from the river to the cliff.

**4** Tell about something that will <u>undoubtedly</u> happen tomorrow.

_____

_____

_____

**5** Have you ever <u>underestimated</u> something or someone? Explain what happened.

_____

_____

_____

# Stonehenge: A Riddle

by Mia Lewis

Stonehenge is a circle of tall stones. It is about 80 miles west of London, in England. This circle of stones has fascinated people for thousands of years. There are many other stone circles all over Europe. This one, however, is the most famous.

People study Stonehenge. They write about it. They talk about it. Experts have ideas about who built it. Even so, no one really is sure of who built it, or why.

**Stop** **Think** **Write**

MAIN IDEAS AND DETAILS

**Where is Stonehenge located?**

_____

_____

_____

# Discovering Dates

Archaeologists try to figure out how old ruins are. They dig carefully. They look at the tools the builders used. If the tools are made of stone or bone, the builders probably worked before metal was used.

As people dig, they look for materials that were once part of living things. They look for wood or bone. These can be tested to see how old they are. The digging and the tests have helped scientists figure out when Stonehenge was built. It was a long time ago!

## Stop Think Write

MAIN IDEAS AND DETAILS

**What is the main idea discussed on this page?**

_____

_____

_____

# Three Stages

The stones at Stonehenge no longer stand as they once did. Many are missing. Some have fallen. The ones that are left reveal a lot. They show that Stonehenge was carefully planned and built at a very slow **pace**. It was built over a long period of time.

The stones were set up in three main stages. The stages were many years apart. They are often called Stonehenge I, Stonehenge II, and Stonehenge III. Each stage was different.

**Stop** **Think** **Write**

VOCABULARY

Why might building something like Stonehenge happen at a slow _pace_?

_____

_____

_____

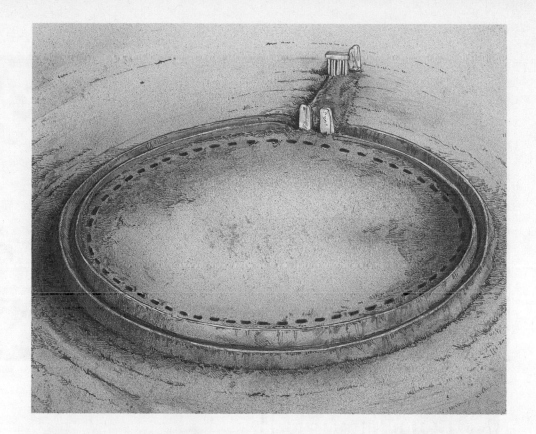

# Stonehenge I

Many people **underestimated** the age of Stonehenge. Archaeologists now think that workers began building about 3100 B.C.E. That's more than 5,000 years ago! They began by digging a round ditch. The ditch, **extending** about twenty feet from side to side, was about six feet deep.

Workers dug fifty-six holes inside the ditch. They filled in the holes with dirt. Nobody is sure what the purpose of the holes was.

## Stop Think Write

MAIN IDEAS AND DETAILS

**Give three details about the first stage of building at Stonehenge.**

_____

_____

_____

## Stonehenge II

The second building stage took place around 2100 B.C.E. Workers put about eighty rocks in the center of the site. These rocks are called bluestones, because of their color.

The bluestones are the smallest rocks at Stonehenge. Still, each one weighs several tons. They probably came from mountains in Wales, about 240 miles away. There were no carts with wheels back then. Maybe the stones were carried over water. Maybe workers used log rollers to drag the stones over land. No one is sure.

**Stop** **Think** **Write**

INFER AND PREDICT

How might using carts with wheels have made moving the stones easier?

_____

_____

_____

# Stonehenge III

More giant stone blocks were added to Stonehenge between 2000 B.C.E. and 1500 B.C.E. Workers built a circle of upright stones. They put a ring of flat stones on top. One flat stone topped each pair of upright stones. Nobody knows exactly how the builders lifted the heavy stones.

In the more recent past, people took stones from Stonehenge to build houses. Now half of the stones are fallen or missing. Even so, Stonehenge is an awesome sight.

## Stop | Think | Write

MAIN IDEAS AND DETAILS

In what special way did builders place stones during the third stage of building at Stonehenge?

_____

_____

_____

# More Questions

Scientists have **reasoned** that Stonehenge was very important in its time. Many workers were needed to carry the stones. Many more were needed to shape the stones and put them up. New rocks were added over a fifteen-hundred-year period.

Maybe the building was for important religious events. Again, no one knows for sure. **Undoubtedly,** people will keep coming up with ideas about Stonehenge. My bet is that the circle of stones will remain a riddle.

## Stop | Think | Write

VOCABULARY

**Write one thing that is <u>undoubtedly</u> true about Stonehenge.**

_____

_____

_____

# Look Back and Respond

**1** How long ago did people first start building at Stonehenge?

_____

_____

_____

**Hint**

For a clue, see page 297.

**2** How far did the people move the bluestones to Stonehenge?

_____

_____

_____

**Hint**

For a clue, see page 298.

**3** How do scientists know that Stonehenge was not just an ordinary building?

_____

_____

_____

**Hint**

For clues, see page 300.

**4** What is the main idea of this selection?

_____

_____

_____

**Hint**

Look through the whole passage.

# Be a Reading Detective!

"Get Lost!"
Student Magazine pp. 66–73

**1** **What is the author's main idea about the maze at Leeds Castle (pages 69–70)?**

☐ It is a very unusual maze.

☐ It is difficult to complete.

☐ It is made from yew trees.

**Prove It!** What evidence in the selection supports your answer?
Check the boxes. ☑ Make notes.

| Evidence | Notes |
|---|---|
| ☐ the first sentence about the maze | |
| ☐ the design of the maze | |
| ☐ the center of the maze | |

**Write About It!**

MAIN IDEAS AND DETAILS

Answer question **1** using evidence from the text.

_____

_____

_____

_____

_____

_____

_____

**2** **What is the difference between a maze and a labyrinth?**

☐ A maze has many paths; a labyrinth has one.

☐ A labyrinth has high walls; a maze has low ones.

☐ A maze is easy to complete; a labyrinth is not.

**Prove It!** What evidence in the selection supports your answer?
Check the boxes. ☑ Make notes.

| Evidence | Notes |
|---|---|
| ☐ information about mazes | |
| ☐ information about labyrinths | |
| ☐ photos | |

**Write About It!**

COMPARE AND CONTRAST

Answer question **2** using evidence from the text.

_____

_____

_____

_____

_____

_____

# Summarize Strategy

When you **summarize**, briefly retell the important ideas in a text.

- Use your own words.

- Organize ideas in a way that makes sense.

- Do not change the meaning of the text.

- Make your summary short. Use only a few sentences.

When you **paraphrase**, restate the author's words in a new way. A paraphrase can be about as long as the text.

- Use synonyms.

- Change the order of words in a sentence.

- Combine sentences. Put related ideas together.

# Analyze/Evaluate Strategy

You can **analyze** and **evaluate** a text. Study the text carefully. Then form an opinion about it.

1.  Analyze the text. Look at the ideas. Think about what the author tells you.
    - What are the important facts and details?

    - How are the ideas organized?

    - What does the author want you to know?

2.  Evaluate the text. Decide what is important. Then form an opinion.
    - How do you feel about what you read?

    - Do you agree with the author's ideas?

    - Did the author succeed in reaching his or her goals?

# Infer/Predict Strategy

You can make an **inference**. Figure out what the author does not tell you.

- Think about the clues in the text.

- Think about what you already know.

You can make a **prediction**. Use text clues to figure out what will happen next.

# Monitor/Clarify Strategy

You can **monitor** what you read. Pay attention to how well you understand the text.

If you read a part that doesn't make sense, find a way to **clarify** it. Clear up what you don't understand.

- Use what you already know.

- Reread or read ahead. Find clues in the text.

- Read more slowly.

- Ask questions about the text.

# Question Strategy

Ask yourself **questions** before, during, and after you read. Look for answers.

Some questions to ask:
- What does the author mean here?

- Who or what is this about?

- Why did this happen?

- What is the main idea?

- How does this work?

# Visualize Strategy

You can **visualize** as you read. Use text details to make pictures in your mind.
- Use the author's words and your own knowledge to help.

- Make mental pictures of people, places, things, actions, and ideas.

## PHOTO CREDITS

Placement Key: (r) right, (l) left, (c) center, (t) top, (b) bottom, (bg) background

blind ii (l) © Pakhnyushchyy/Fotolia. blind iii (r) Comstock/Getty Images. 2 (b) © Stockbyte/Getty Images. 2 (t) © Artville. 3 (t) © Shutterstock. 3 (bl) © PhotoDisc, Inc. 3 (br) © Artville. 4 © Classic Pio Images. 5 © Stockbyte/Getty Images. 5 (tr) © Getty Images/PhotoDisc. 5 (bl) © Getty Images/PhotoDisc. 6 © PhotoDisc, Inc. 7 (t) © Brand X Pictures. 7 (bl) © Artville/Getty Images. 7 (pen & pencil) © Artville. 7 (c) © Artville. 8 © Getty Images/PhotoDisc. 9 © PhotoDisc, Inc. 10 © Getty Images/PhotoDisc. 11A (b) Walter Hodges/Digital Vision/Getty Images. 11B (b) ©Tetra Images/Superstock. 12 © UpperCut Images/Alamy Images. 12 Comstock/Jupiterimages/Getty Images. 13 Jupiterimages/Getty Images. 14 Comstock/Getty Images. 14 Dynamic Graphics/Getty Images. 15 Getty Images/PhotoDisc. 15 Ryan McVay/Photodisc/Getty Images. 17 © Photodisc/Alamy. 17 Comstock/Getty Images. 18 Comstock/Getty Images. 18 Photodisc/Getty Images. 19 Comstock/Getty Images. 19 Photodisc/Getty Images. 20 Getty Images/PhotoDisc. 20 Photodisc/Getty Images. 20 Comstock/Getty Images. 21A (c) © Getty Images. 21B (c) Sami Sarkis/Photodisc/Getty Images. 22 © Artville. 23 (t) © Photodisc. 23 (b) © Getty Images/PhotoDisc. 24 (b) © Image Ideas. 24 (t) © Getty Images. 25 © PhotoDisc, Inc. 26 © Shutterstock. 27 © Getty Images/PhotoDisc. 28–29 (t) © Artville. 28 (bl) © Comstock. 28 (br) © PhotoDisc. 29 © Comstock. 30 © Getty Images/PhotoDisc. 30 (b) © Comstock. 31 © Getty Images/PhotoDisc. 31A (c) Stockdisc/Getty Images. 32 (t) © Stockbyte. 32 (b) © Corbis. 33 © PhotoDisc, Inc. 42 (tl) © Comstock, Inc. 42 (bl) © Artville. 42 (br) © Artville. 42 (tr) © PhotoDisc, Inc. 43 © Getty Images/PhotoDisc. 44 © Artville. 45 © Getty Images/PhotoDisc. 47 (tl) © Artville. 47 (bl) © PhotoDisc, Inc. 47 (pen & pencil) © Artville. 47 (r) © Artville/Getty Images. 48 (tl) © Artville. 48–49 © PhotoDisc, Inc. 48 (tape) © Artville. 48 (sharpener) © Artville. 50 (t) © Artville. 50 © PhotoDisc, Inc. 51 © Artville. 51A (cl) © Malcolm Schuyl/Alamy Images. 51B (cr) © David Newham/Alamy Images. 52 Getty Images/Photodisc. 53 Getty Images/Photodisc. 53 Stockbyte/Getty Images. 54 Fotolia. 54 Martin Ruegner/Getty Images. 55 © D. Hurst/Alamy. 55 Creativ Studio Heinemann/Getty Images. 56 © Adam Jones/Digital Vision/Getty Images. 56 Photodisc/Getty Images. 58 © Tony Sweet/Getty Images. 60 Jack Hollingsworth/Photodisc/Getty Images. 61 © D. Hurst/Alamy. 61 Creativ Studio Heinemann/Getty Images. 61A (b) © Digital Vision/Getty Images. 61B (cr) © Getty Images. 62 © PhotoDisc, Inc. 63 (t) © Digital Vision/Getty Images. 63 (c) © PhotoDisc/Getty Images. 63 (b) © Shutterstock. 64–70 (border) © Getty Images/PhotoDisc. 71A (b) © Richard Wear/Design Pics/Corbis. 72 © PhotoDisc, Inc. 73 © Dynamic. 74–75 © Getty Images/PhotoDisc. 75 (r) © Getty Images. 76 (t) © Getty Images/PhotoDisc. 76–77 © Getty Images/PhotoDisc. 77 (l) © Getty Images. 77 (c) © Stockbyte/Getty Images. 77 (r) © Corbis. 78–79 © Getty Images/PhotoDisc. 79 (bl) © Shutterstock. 79 (tl) © PhotoDisc, Inc. 79 (tr) © PhotoDisc, Inc. 79 (br) © Image Ideas. 80 (bg) © Getty Images/PhotoDisc. 80 (t) © Getty Images. 80 (c) © Stockbyte/Getty Images. 80 (b) © Getty Images/PhotoDisc. 81 © Getty Images/PhotoDisc. 81A (b) © Comstock/Corbis. 82 © Getty Images. 83 (b) © PhotoDisc, Inc. 83 (t) © Comstock. 84–85 © PhotoDisc, Inc. 85 (radio) © Comstock. 86–87 (bg) © Digital Vision/Getty Images. 86 © Shutterstock. 87 © Comstock. 88–89 (bg) © Digital Vision/Getty Images. 88 © Comstock. 89 © Digital Stock. 90 (bg) © Getty Images. 90 © Comstock. 91 © Shutterstock. 91A (b) Jupiterimages/Getty Images. 92 (c) © PhotoDisc, Inc. 92 (b) © Shutterstock. 92 (t) © PhotoDisc, Inc. 93 © PhotoDisc, Inc. 101A (b) © Paul Edmondson/Photodisc/Getty Images. 101B (bc) © Gaertner/Alamy Images. 102 (t) © Eyewire. 102 (b) © Stockbyte. 103 © PhotoDisc, Inc. 108 © Comstock, Inc. 109 © Comstock, Inc. 111A (b) Jupiterimages/Getty Images. 111B (cr) © Fotolia. 112 (l) © PhotoDisc, Inc. 112 © Artville. 113 © PhotoDisc, Inc. 121 © PhotoDisc, Inc. 121A (b) Library of Congress. 121B (c) © Ocean/Corbis. 122 © Getty Images/PhotoDisc. 123 © Eyewire. 125 (tl) © Digital Stock. 125 (tr) © Getty Images/PhotoDisc. 125 (c) © Stockbyte/Getty Images. 125 (b) © PhotoDisc, Inc. 127 © Getty Images/PhotoDisc. 128 (t) © Stockbyte/Getty Images. 128 (b) © Eyewire. 129 (t) © Shutterstock. 129 (br) © Comstock. 129 (keys) © PhotoDisc, Inc. 129 (viewer) © Artville. 129 (bl) © Comstock. 129 (c) © Getty Images/PhotoDisc. 130 (bg) © Digital Stock. 130 (b) © PhotoDisc, Inc. 130 (t) © Getty Images/PhotoDisc. 131 © Getty Images/PhotoDisc. 131B (bc) Brand X Pictures/Getty Images. 131B (b) Getty Images/Photodisc. 133 © PhotoDisc, Inc. 141A (c) Comstock/Getty Images. 142 © Corbis. 144 (b) © Brand X Pictures. 144 (t) © Corbis. 145 © PhotoDisc, Inc. 148 © Artville. 151A (b) Surrender of Lord Cornwallis (1820), John Trumbull. Oil on canvas, 12' x 18'. Architect of the Capitol. 152 © PhotoDisc, Inc. 153 © PhotoDisc, Inc. 154 (curtain) © Comstock. 154–155 © PhotoDisc, Inc. 156 (t) © PhotoDisc, Inc. 156 (b) © Artville. 157–159 © PhotoDisc, Inc. 160 (t) © Artville. 160 (bl) © Artville. 160 (br) © PhotoDisc, Inc.